THE FACSIMILE TEXT SOCIETY

SERIES I: LITERATURE AND LANGUAGE

VOLUME 4

CLARA REEVE

THE PROGRESS OF ROMANCE

1785

CLARA REEVE

THE PROGRESS OF ROMANCE

AND THE HISTORY OF CHAROBA,
QUEEN OF AEGYPT

Reproduced from the Colchester Edition of 1785

With a Bibliographical Note
by
ESTHER M. McGILL

THE FACSIMILE TEXT SOCIETY

NEW YORK

1930

Printed in the United States of America
by The National Process Company, New York

BIBLIOGRAPHICAL NOTE

Two editions of *The Progress of Romance*
appeared in 1785 — one published in Colchester, 8vo, the other in Dublin, 12mo.
There are no later editions. The present one
is reprinted from the copy of the Colchester
edition now in the Library of Congress.

The History of Charoba, Queen of Egypt,
an oriental tale which also appears in this
volume, was printed with both editions of *The
Progress of Romance.* This is Clara Reeve's
adaptation of a story in the history of ancient
Egypt by Murtadhā ibn al-Khafīf. It had
been published in 1672 as *The Egyptian History, treating of the Pyramids, the inundation
of the Nile and other prodigies, according to
the opinions and traditions of the Arabians:
written . . . in the Arabian tongue by Murtadi
. . . rendered into French* [with a Preface]
*by Mons. Vattier . . . and thence faithfully
done into English by J. Davies.* Mrs. Reeve
not only modernized the language of the tale
as it appeared in Davies' translation, but she
altered the story itself. The tale assumes an
added interest as the immediate source of
Landor's *Gebir.*

E. M. McG.

Columbia University
   July, 1930

THE
PROGRESS *of* ROMANCE,

THROUGH

TIMES, COUNTRIES, AND MANNERS;

WITH

REMARKS

ON THE GOOD AND BAD EFFECTS OF
IT, ON THEM RESPECTIVELY;

IN A COURSE OF

EVENING CONVERSATIONS.

BY C. R. AUTHOR OF

Clara Reeve

THE ENGLISH BARON, THE TWO MENTORS, &.

IN TWO VOLUMES.

VOL. I.

It hath bene through all ages ever seene,
That with the praise of armes and chevalrie
The prize of beautie still hath ioyned beene,
And that for reasons speciall privitee,
For either doth on other much relie :
For he me seemes most fit the faire to serve,
That can her best defend from villenie,
And she most fit his service doth deserve,
That fairest is, and from her faith will never swerve.

SPENSER's Faery Queene. Book 4. Canto 5. Stanza 1.

PRINTED FOR THE AUTHOR,
BY W. KEYMER, COLCHESTER, AND SOLD BY HIM;
SOLD ALSO BY G. G. J. AND J. ROBINSON,
IN PATER-NOSTER ROW, LONDON.
MDCCLXXXV.

PREFACE.

ROMANCES may not improperly be called the polite literature of early ages, and they have been the favourite amusements of later times. In rude and barbarous ages, they resided in the breath of oral tradition, in civilized nations they were of course committed to writing: and in still more polished periods, they have varied their forms, and have appeared either in prose or verse, according to the genius of the writers, or the taste of the times.

In

In the following pages, I have endeavoured to trace the progrefs of this
fpecies of compofition, through all its
fucceffive ftages and variations, to point
out its moft ftriking effects and influence
upon the manners, and to affift according
to my beft judgment, the reader's choice,
amidft the almoft infinite variety it affords, in a felection of fuch as are moft
worthy of a place in the libraries of
readers of every clafs, who feek either
for information or entertainment.

How far I have fucceeded in this attempt, muft now be left to the decifion
of that tribunal which I have ever
approached with the moft refpectful
diffidence; and whofe indulgence, I am
perhaps in the prefent inftance concerned more than ever to implore.

While many eminent writers have (if
I may be permitted the allufion) fkim-
med over the furface of this fubject, it
                          feemed

seemed to me that none of them had founded the depths of it.——Of metrical Romances they have treated largely, but with respect to those in prose, their informations have been scanty and imperfect.

When they approach that period of obscurity, which began with the spreading of Christianity over the western world, they drop entirely the latter and equally essential branch of the subject; nor do they resume it, till the sixteenth Century, when *Calprenede*, the *Scuderies*, *D'Urfé*, and other French writers, revived the taste for prose Romances, by their productions.

To fill up this chasm in the history of Romance, to rectify the mistakes that have been made by indiscriminate praise or blame, to methodise and arrange the works themselves, and to ascertain as many of the Authors, and the dates of

A 3   them

them as I could get information of, to mark the diſtinguiſhing characters of the Romance and the Novel, to point out the boundaries of both : and laſtly to preſent to the reader's eye a ſelection of the beſt writings of both kinds.

Theſe objects would I thought, have a fair claim to the attention of the public ; and if executed with fidelity and judgment, would I hoped merit its approbation and encouragement.

While I was collecting materials for this work, I held many converſations with ſome ingenious friends upon the various ſubjects, which it offered to be inveſtigated and explained. This circumſtance naturally ſuggeſted to me the Idea of the dialogue form ; in which oppoſite ſentiments would admit of a more full and accurate examination, arguments and objections might be more clearly ſtated and diſcuſſed, than in a

regular

regular series of Essays, or even letters, not to mention, that the variety and contrast which naturally arise out of the Dialogue, might enliven a work of rather dry deduction, and render it more entertaining to the reader, and not the less useful or instructive.—In this Idea I was confirmed by the great success of some late writers in this way, particularly of *Madame de Genlis*, in her excellent work called the *Theatre of Education*.

It was not till I had compleated my design, that I read either Dr. *Beattie*'s *Dissertation on Fable and Romance*, or Mr. *Warton*'s *History of English Poetry*.—To the perusal of these books, I was most strongly recommended by two friends, to whom I had shewn my own work, and to whose judgment I owe all possible respect and deference.—I obeyed their injunctions, and have additional

A 4   obligations

obligations to them for the entertainment afforded me by these excellent writers —I soon found that they neither interfered with my plan, nor had anticipated my subject, yet I own I was well pleased, that neither of these books had fallen in my way before I had finished my own work; as otherwise it might have been supposed that I had borrowed my lights from them, where ever there happened to be a concurrence of opinion, or of representation.

Dr. *Beattie* has walked over the ground, aud marked out its boundaries, but he has paid little attention to its various produce, whether of flowers, herbs, or weeds; except a very few works of capital merit, (some of which he confesses he had not read through) he consigns all the rest to oblivion. Thus Genius thinks it enough to strike out the outline, and leaves to industry and

inferior

inferior talents, the minuter parts, and more laborious tafk of detail and arrangement.

From Mr. *Warton*'s *Hiftory of Englifh Poetry*, I might indeed have derived confiderable advantages, had I met with it fooner. I was happy however to find, that in many inftances, my opinions were confirmed, and my arguments ftrengthened by this learned and judicious writer.

It had long been a received opinion, that Romances were communicated to the Weftern world by the Crufades.— Mr. *Warton* allows that they were introduced at a much earlier period, viz. by the Saracens; who came from Africa, and fettled in Spain, about the beginning of the eighth Century.—From Spain he imagines, they found an eafy paffage into France and Italy.—He further examines the *Hypothefes* of Dr. *Percy* and Mr.

Mallet;

Mallet; who derive thefe fictions from the ancient fongs of the Gothic Bards and Scalds: this Idea he allows to be well founded, fo far at leaft as it does not exclude his own Syftem.—Thefe fictions (he fays) had taken deep root in Europe, and prepared the way for the *Arabian* fables which were introduced in the ninth Century, by which they were in a great meafure fuperfeded.

That Chivalry, which was the fub-ftance of Romance, exifted among the Goths he allows, but adds, that under the Feudal eftablifhment, it received new ftrength and vigour: and was invefted with the formalities of a regular infti-tution —Which Dr. *Percy* likewife ac-knowledges in his remarks on Chivalry; the paffage is quoted in the body of this work.—Mr. *Warton* next proceeds to the Minftrels, Troubadours, and early poets of this country, which is his pro-

per fubject; it was entirely befide his
plan to enter further into the fubject of
profe Romances.

It is remarkable, that among the many learned and ingenious writers who
have treated this fubject, few have taken proper notice of the Greek Romances, which may juftly be deemed
the parents of all the reft. The learned
men of our own country, have in general
affected a contempt for this kind of
writing, and looked upon Romances, as
proper furniture only for a lady's Library.—Not fo the French and Italian writ-
ters, on the contrary they have not only
deemed them worthy their own attention; but have laboured to make them
deferving of ours.

I mean not however to include all the
learned of our country under this obfervation.—The names of *Hurd, Beattie,
Warton, Percy,* and *Mallet,* are an honourable

nourable exception, a fubject that has been thought worthy of any portion of their time and attention, cannot be undeferving the notice and protection of the public. It is with fincere pleafure I add a name that will not difgrace the lift, a writer of my own fex, Mrs. *Dobfon* the elegant writer of the *Hiftory of the Troubadours* and the *Memoirs of Ancient Chivalry.*

In anfwer to fome objections, made by a learned writer, whofe friendfhip does me honour, to my account of the antiquity of Romance-writing; I was led to afk him, why the fictions of the Ægyptians and Arabians, of the Greeks and Romans, were not entitled to the appellations of Romances, as well as thofe of the middle ages, to which it was generally appropriated?—I was anfwered by another queftion.—What did I know of the Romances of thofe countries?

tries?—Had I ever feen an Ægyptian
Romance? I replied, yes, and I would
fhortly give him a proof of it. I ac-
cordingly compiled and methodifed the
Hiftory of Charoba Queen of Ægypt.—
My friend was furprifed and puzzled,
and anfwered me to this effect.

" I return your Ægyptian ftory with
" thanks; whence you took it, or how
" far it is your own I know not."—As
I think this piece a great literary curiofity, I fhall give it to the public, at the
end of this work.—That I may not appear to claim a right to the invention of
this ftory, I fhall inform my readers
from whence it is taken.—It is extracted
from a book called—*The Hiftory of An-*
cient Ægypt, according to the Traditions
of the Arabians.—*Written in Arabic, by*
the Reverend Doctor Murtadi, the Son
of Gapiphus, the Son of Chatem, the Son
of Molfem the Macdefian.—*Tranflated in-*
to

*to French by M. Vattier, Arabic Pro-
feſſor to Louis 14th King of France.*

This tranſlator in his Preface ſpeaks
of this ſtory in high terms " Were
" there nothing in this ſtory (ſays he)
" worthy of our notice but the Fable
" of Gebirus and Charoba, with the
" Adventure of the Shepherd, and the
" Sea-nymph, I ſhould not repent of
" my trouble in this Tranſlation.—I
" little thought to find in an Arabian
" writer, a ſtory ſo nearly reſembling
" the fables of the Greek and Latin
" poets.—While I was writing, it fre-
" quently reminded me of the 4th book
" of the Odyſſey, and of ſeveral parts
" of *Ovid*'s *Metamorphoſes.*

This ſtory is mentioned in the ingenious Mrs. *Rowe*'s *Hiſtory of Joſeph,* a
poem not ſo much known and valued
as it deſerves to be.—I truſt that my
readers will not be diſpleaſed with a
quotation from it.   When

When Totis by his death, the fole command
Of Mifraim left to fair Charoba's hand;
The rich Gebirus from Chaldea came
With foreign pomp to feek the royal dame.
Chemis adorn'd his train, whofe beauteous face
Allur'd a goddefs of the watery race;
On Nilus' banks the young Chaldean ftood,
When Io Marina rifing from the flood!
Her chariot fet with pearl, the wave divides,
Softly along the filver ftream fhe glides,
Her robes with fparkling gems tranfparent fhine,
Her brighter Eyes exprefs a light divine;
Not from her humid bed the blooming day
Has e'er afcended with a brighter ray.
She leaves her Chryftal vaults and coral groves
And o'er the graffy meads with Chemis roves.
At parting gave him a celeftial fpell
Which every good procures, and ills expel
My mother from this pair derives her line
And this fhe left me, as a gift divine,
By all her Anceftors preferv'd with Care;
One drop of this fhall banifh all defpair.

Mrs. ROWE's HIST. OF JOSEPH, Book 6th.

This curious ftory will fufficiently
anfwer my purpofe, if it only furnifhes
an additional proof that Romances are
of univerfal growth, and not confined
to

to any particular period or countries. They were the delight of barbarous ages, and they have always kept their ground amongft the multiplied amufements of more refined and cultivated periods, containing like every other branch of human literature, both good and evil things.   They are not to be put into the hands of young perfons without diftinction and reserve, but under proper reftrictions and regulations they will afford much ufeful inftruction, as well as rational and elegant amufement.   In this view therefore they are equally entitled to our attention and refpect, as any other works of Genius and literature.

PROGRES

PROGRESS of ROMANCE.

EVENING I.

Hortenſius, Sophronia, Euphraſia.

Euph. HORTENSIUS, I am proud of a viſit from you, tho' I am ignorant of the motive to which I am indebted for it.

Hort. What Madam, do you think you can give a challenge, and go off with impunity?—I am come hither to demand an explanation of your behaviour laſt Thurſday evening at *Sophronia's* houſe; and I have brought her with me to be a witneſs to our diſpute—of the defeat of one of us,—or perhaps of our compromiſe, and reconciliation.

Soph. Or that *Euphraſia* ſhall make a convert to her own opinion.

Euph. I am obliged to the occasion that brings you both to spend an hour with me.—Pray be seated my friends, and let me understand your meaning.—Surely I was not so presumptuous as to challenge *Hortensius?*

Hort. I will not suffer you either by raillery or compliment to evade my purpose.—In the course of our late conversation, you threw out several hints that struck me as either *new,* or *uncommon,* in respect to the works of the ancient and modern writers;—but what surprised me most of all, you seemed to degrade Epic poetry, and to place it on an equality with the old Romance. I wish you to explain your sentiments on this head, for I cannot account for your defence of a kind of writings that are generally exploded. I little expected to hear *Euphrasia* ridicule the works of the great Ancients.—(You smile) —Yes Madam, raillery was the only weapon you deigned to use, in opposition to my arguments.—Yet you told me you had better reasons in reserve, but you did not choose then to enter upon the subject, as it would engross too much of our time and attention.

Euph.

Euph. Your memory Sir, is very retentive, and there is no warding off your attack; perhaps I only seemed to degrade your favourites, and exalt the others, becaufe I oppofed opinions long received, and but little examined; while in reality I only meant to place each in their proper rank, both as to merit and utility.

Hort. To convince me of that, you muft give me a full explanation of your opinions in refpect to both, and alfo of the foundation of them.

Soph. I have promifed in your behalf that you fhall give *Hortenfius* full fatisfaction, and my honour is engaged for it—I know this is a fubject you are not unprepared to fpeak upon.

Euph. Methinks you demand no trifling fatisfaction for my Challenge, as it pleafes you to call it. However I fhall not refufe to comply with your requeft, if you can have patience to liften, while I inveftigate a fubject of greater extent than perhaps you may fuppofe, and which though I am not quite unprepared for, I am afraid to begin.

Soph.

Soph. My dear friend, it is your patience and not ours that will be tried. I am very defirous to hear this subject difcuffed, and to be informed by the converfation of two fuch opponents. I expect from *Euphrafia*'s reading and obfervation much advantage to myfelf.

Hort. My expectations Madam, do not fall fhort of yours.

Euph. No compliments my good friends! my reading and obfervations are very much at your fervice, I wifh they may afford you information or entertainment. I will confefs to you that I have confidered this fubject deeply, and that I have written fome remarks upon it.—I have made many extracts from different Authors, and collected materials of various kinds; always intending to methodize them one time or other.—I will bring my papers before you, communicate my remarks, propofe my opinions; and either be confirmed in them by your approbation, or be filenced by your better arguments on the contrary fide;—perhaps I may be enabled to
ftrike

ſtrike out new lights upon the ſubject, when
my imagination is corrected by the judgment of *Hortenſius*.

Hort. No compliments I repeat. I wiſh I
may be able to ſtand my ground. I find you
are making great preparations againſt me,
you are coming upon me armed with your
papers and extracts.—Artillery and fire-arms
againſt the ſmall ſword, the tongue.

Euph. A moſt warlike alluſion! and the
compariſon holds good; for if I ſhould come
to a cloſe engagement, the ſmall ſword will
deſtroy what may eſcape the artillery.

Hort. Fairly replied.—The attack is begun, I have queſtioned you cloſely, it is your
part to maintain your own opinions. You
have ſaid that Romances are neither ſo contemptible, nor ſo dangerous a kind of reading, as they are generally repreſented—you
have compared them to Epic-poems.

Euph. Let me firſt entreat you my good
friends to diveſt yourſelves of common prejudices:—excuſe the expreſſion.—Mankind
in general are more biaſſed by names than

things

things; and what is yet ſtranger, they are biaſſed by names to which they have not affixed an abſolute and determinate meaning. —For inſtance—pray what do you underſtand by the word Romance?

Hort. By Romance I underſtand a wild, extravagant, fabulous Story.

Euph. *Sophronia*, favour me with an explanation of this word? It is not merely a queſtion of idle curioſity.

Soph. I underſtand it to mean all thoſe kind of ſtories that are built upon fiction, and have no foundation in truth.

Euph. You will pleaſe to reflect, that under this general denomination of Romance, a vaſt genus of compoſition is included, works of various kinds, merits, and tendencies. It is running ſome hazard, to praiſe or to decry in general terms, without being perfectly acquainted with the whole extent of the ſubject under conſideration.

Hort. What is it neceſſary to read all the traſh contained in this Genus, as it pleaſes you to call it, in order to ſpeak of any part of it ?

Euph.

Euph. By no means, I will explain this point prefently.—No writings are more different than the ancient *Romance* and modern *Novel,* yet they are frequently confounded together, and miftaken for each other. There are likewife great diftinctions to be made between the *old Greek* Romances, thofe of the middle ages, and thofe of the fifteenth and fixteenth Centuries. Books of all thefe kinds have been enthufiaftically read and admired; of late years they have been as abfurdly cenfured and condemned. If read indifcriminately they are at beft unprofitable, frequently productive of abfurdities in manners and fentiments, fometimes hurtful to good morals; and yet from this Genus there may be felected books that are truly refpectable, works of genius, tafte, and utility, capable of improving the morals and manners of mankind.

Soph. I am entirely of your opinion, and give my teftimony to this truth.

Euph. It feems to me that this Genus of compofition has never been properly diftin-

guifhed

guifhed or afcertained; that it wants to be methodized, to be feparated, claffed, und regulated; and that a work of this kind would be both entertaining and ufeful.

Soph. Doubtlefs it would, and you give us hopes of feeing this accomplifhed.

Hort. I perceive that you are laying a deep foundation, but what kind of building you will raife upon it, I am impatient to hear.

Euph. If you will honour me with your attention, and fometimes give me your afiftance, we will at leifure hours purfue this fubject together. Let me befpeak your favour, by affuring you that I mean to do fomething more than merely to invefligate *names* :—we will afterwards proceed to confider the beauties and defects of thefe writings, of the ufes and abufes, and of their effects upon the manners of the times in which they were written. I propofe to trace Romance to its Origin, to follow its progrefs through the different periods to its declenfion, to fhew how the modern Novel fprung up out of its ruins, to examine and compare the merits of both, and to remark upon the effects of them.

Hort.

Hort. Upon my word you do well to lay a deep foundation, the superstructure will require it: if it be well executed it will do you honour, and without a compliment, I think you equal to this undertaking.

Euph. You may be mistaken, and yet I may be entitled to your allowance,—the design may be good though the execution should fall short. I always mean more than I can express;—my materials increase upon me, insomuch that I fear I may be encumbered by the number and variety of them. I shall depend upon your assistance, and since you have opened my mouth upon the subject, you are bound in honour to correct my redundancies, and to supply my deficiencies.

Hort. What to furnish you with weapons for my defeat?

Euph. Not so, but to assist me in the course of my progress through the land of Romance. I purpose to remark upon the most eminent works of the kind, and to pay the tribute of praise to works of Genius and morality.

Hort.

Hort. I refpect both the motive and the end too much to difcourage you, and you may depend upon every affiftance in my power.

Euph. Let then the prefent converfation ferve as an introduction to our progrefs, the next time we meet we will purfue the fub-ject more clofely.

Hort. Let it be at my houfe next Thurf-day ladies!

Soph. Agreed, and let the Thurfday in every week be fet apart for this purpofe, till the progrefs is finifhed.

Euph. With all my heart.—I will readily attend you in turn.

Hort. I am much obliged to you, for your readinefs to gratify my curiofity, and fhall expect next Thurfday with fome impatience. —adieu Madam.

Euph. I fhall depend upon you for encou-ragement when deferved,—correction where

I am miftaken, and allowance where wanted. —adieu my friends.

EVENING

EVENING II.

Hortensius, Sophronia, Euphrasia.

Hort. LADIES, I rejoice to see you at my house on this occasion. Let us lay aside form and ceremony, and proceed to the business of our meeting.—I expect a pitch'd battle; for I see *Euphrasia* has brought her artillery and is placing them to advantage.

Euph. You know your advantages, and that a woman is your opponent.

Hort. Whether you mean me a compliment or reproof, is not clear.—But I will not reply to it, lest it should hinder business. —It lies upon you Madam to proceed with your investigation.

Soph.

Soph. You are to explain to us the word Romance, of which it seems we have no certain Idea.

Euph. Since our laſt meeting I have not been idle.—I have conſulted all the Dictionary writers upon the ſubjeſt, and I do not find that any of them are clear and certain in their definition of it.

Ainſworth and *Littleton* ſpeak in the following terms :—*Narratio fiſta,—fabuloſa heroicorum facinorum hiſtoria.—Scriptum eroticum—ſplendida fabula.*

Boyer calls a Romance too conciſely—*un fable—une conte—an menſonge.*

Old *Dyche* and *Bailey*—a fiſtion, or feigned Story.

Dr. *Johnſon*—a military fable of the *middle ages :*—A tale of wild adventures of war and love.

With all reſpeſt to the Doſtor's judgment,—I muſt affirm that this definition can only be proper to the Romances of the middle ages, but cannot extend to the whole Genus.

Hort.

Hort. A proper diftinction—but what ufe will you make of it?

Euph. The Origin of Romance is of much higher date, as I hope to convince you,—but firft let us fpeak of the name.

Hort. How then would you define it?

Euph. By fixing a clear and certain meaning to it, not as of my own invention or judgment; but borrowing the idea of the Latinifts, I would call it fimply an *Heroic fable*,—a fabulous Story of fuch actions as are commonly afcribed to heroes, or men of extraordinary courage and abilites.—Or if you would allow of it, I would fay an Epic in profe.

Hort. I cannot allow of the laft appellation, but to the firft I make no objection. An Epic is a very fuperior compofition.

Euph. We will fpeak of that hereafter. I do not defpair of bringing you over to my definition; but let us firft trace the Origin of our fubject.   Romances or Heroic fables are of very ancient, and I might fay univerfal Origin. We find traces of them in all times, and

and in all countries : they have always been
the favourite entertainment of the moſt ſa-
vage, as well as the moſt civilized people. In
the earlieſt accounts of all nations, we find
they had traditional ſtories of their moſt eminent perſons, that is of their *Heroes*, to which
they liſtened in raptures, and found themſelves excited to perform great actions, by
hearing them recited ;—they had their war-
ſongs—and they had alſo their proſe narra-
tives.

Hort. This is indeed a truth that cannot
be denied, I did not expect ſo ancient, nor ſo
well authenticated an Origin, as you have
given them.

Soph. I knew that *Euphraſia* would never
advance, what ſhe could not defend,—proceed Madam.

Euph. As a country became civilized, their
narrations were methodized, and moderated
to probability.—From the proſe recitals
ſprung Hiſtory,—from the war-ſongs Romance and Epic poetry.

Hort. Hiſtory—Romance—and Epics all
in a breath !

Euph.

Euph. Let us firſt diſtinguiſh Hiſtory from
the others.——When a nation became acquainted with letters, they could record facts, and
this is the Æra of true Hiſtory.   Before that
time a ſtory, that at firſt was founded on facts,
by length of time and paſſing through many
hands, loſt many real circumſtances, and acquired many fictitious ones.   The heathen
Mythology is an unanſwerable proof of this
truth;—— what at firſt was the Hiſtory of mortal men, and their actions, was at length aſ-
cribed to deities;   and the veil of Allegory
concealed and altered facts, till they could no
longer be traced, and at laſt were loſt in fable
and obſcurity.   Theſe Stories, though no
longer believed by wiſe men as truths, yet
continued to pleaſe as agreeable fictions;
and in more enlightened times, men of Genius and fancy, perceiving the pleaſure they
gave and how willingly they were received,
imitated thoſe antient fables, and in proceſs
of time compoſed others of different kinds,
following the track of their talents, and the
temper of the times in which they lived.

Hort.

Hort. All this I allow.—But will you in-
volve Hiſtory in this obſcurity?

Euph. By no means.—Let us now leave
Hiſtory to her own ſtrength and evidence, as
the nobleſt and moſt uſeful of all ſtudies;
and let us proceed to Romance, and the Epic
poem.

Hort. Romance aud Epic again!—do you
affirm that they are the ſame?

Euph. I do affirm it, and will endeavour
to maintain it. They ſpring from the ſame
root,—they deſcribe the ſame actions and
circumſtances,—they produce the ſame ef_
fects, and they are continually miſtaken for
each other.

Hort. Your pardon Madam,—·I muſt mention one material difference —The Epic
poem is always derived from ſome Hiſtorical
fact, though perhaps remote and obſcure.

Euph. Remote and obſcure indeed.—So
perhaps are ſome of the ſtories in *Ovid*'s
Metamorphoſes,—but I will bring a fairer
compariſon.—In the French Romances of the
ſixteenth Century, they had their foundation
in

in real Hiſtory; but the ſuperſtructure was pure fiction. I will not ſhelter myſelf under their authority, I will not ſpeak of them as reſpectable works.—Let us con promiſe.—If you will permit me to go on in my own way, perhaps I may anſwer your objections when you leaſt expect it, and I ſhall call upon you to make them, in due time.

Hort. I will hear you with attention and impartiality: but I wiſh you to come to the point directly.

Soph. The diſpute waxes warm.—My dear *Euphraſia,* I expect you to anſwer all the ſcruples of *Hortenſius.*

Euph. Well then, I will come to the point you wiſh to bring me.—Mankind willingly adopt the prejudices of their anceſtors, they embrace them with affection, they quit them with reluctance. One of them is to decry Romance, and venerate Epic Poetry. I believe *Hortenſius* has as few prejudices as any man living; but I muſt think this to be a ſtrong one, and as ſuch I ſhall treat it, and endeavour to cure him of it.

Hort.

Hort. I hope I am open to conviction, and ready to acknowledge truth, whether it makes for or against me.—Proceed Madam.

Euph. The Romances of all countries are derived from the bards. All countries have had their bards of early times, and their prose Romances afterwards.—Lest my opinion should not be sufficient, I shall refer you to Dr. *Percy's* Essay on the old *Metrical Romances*, in which he has treated this subject, in so clear and judicious a manner, that nothing I can say is worthy to come after it.—You shall take it home with you, and it will prepare you for our next conversation. You will there find that Romances have been written both in prose and verse, and that according to the different circumstances of the Author's genius and situation, they became Epics or Romances.

Hort. I will certainly read it, but I will not promise to receive it implicitly.—I cannot with any patience see *Homer* and *Virgil* degraded into writers of Romances.

Euph.

Euph. I would not willingly degrade thofe great Poets: but I beg leave to diftinguifh them.———

Homer is univerfally acknowledged as the Prince of Epic poetry. If we may believe Dr. *Blackwell*, there was a wonderful concurrence of circumftances, that elevated him to this high ftation; circumftances unlikely, perhaps impoffible, to happen again to any other Poet, or at leaft as improbable, as to find another Poet equally capable of ufing the fame advantages:—but with all this eclat that furrounds him, *Homer* was the parent of Romance; where ever his works have been known, they have been imitated by the Poets and Romance writers.—I look upon *Virgil* as the moft fuccefsful of his Imitators.

Hort. This is what I call degrading both thefe divine men, which I did not expect from you, whom I reckoned among their admirers.

Euph. I am fo ftill, as much as poffible, on this fide Idolatry.—I venerate *Homer* as much as one unlearned in his own language can do. From *Pope*'s admired tranflation I can difcern

C 2

cern

cern the strong paintings of his bold imagination, his knowledge and judgment in marking his characters; and above all things, the consideration that the world owes to him, in a great measure, the knowledge of the History and Manners of the times in which he wrote, and of some ages before him; on these and many other accounts, *Homer* must always claim our respect and even veneration.—But after all this can you forbear smiling at the extravagant sallies of his imagination, can you approve his violent machinery, in which he degrades his deities below his heroes, and makes deities of men. In a word, if you will not smile with me, I know many of his admirers that will; in spite of the labours of his commentators, who strive with all their strength, to allegorize away his absurdities.

Hort. Upon my word Madam, you have made a bold attack, I am not prepared to answer you of a sudden, but I shall do it hereafter.

Euph. In the mean time I am preparing to anticipate your answer, and to obviate your objections.

prejudice

objections.—It is aftonifhing that men of fenfe, and of learning, fhould fo ftrongly imbibe prejudices, and be fo loth to part with them.—That they fhould defpife and ridicule Romances, as the moft contemptible of all kinds of writing, and yet expatiate in raptures, on the beauties of the fables of the old claffic Poets,—on ftories far more wild and extravagant, and infinitely more incredible.

Hort. It is becaufe we pay due refpect to works of true Genius, and difdain the comparifon of fuch weak and paltry imitations, as thofe you have undertaken to fupport.

Euph. I am no ftranger to the charms of Poetry, I have even felt a degree of its enthufiafm, yet I cannot facrifice the convictions of truth at its fhrine. I am of opinion that many of the fine old Hiftorical ballads, are equally entitled to the name of Epic poems.

There are examples enough extant, of Romance in verfe, and Epics in profe. I fhall produce fome of them in the courfe of our progrefs:—but at prefent I fhall only mention the *Provencals,* or *Troubadours,*—and I refer you to Mrs. *Dobfon's* account of them.

Hort.

Hort. You would engage me in a new course of reading, but I had rather you would give me your own arguments.

Euph. I am afraid they fhould not be fufficient, but I will try a fhorter way with you. You think the divine *Homer* degraded by my comparifons, yet I will fhew you a ftriking refemblance of him, in a work of much lower eftimation :—Did you never read a book called the Arabian Nights Entertainments?

Hort. You cannot be in earneft in this comparifon?

Euph. Indeed I am.—If you will take the trouble to read the Story of *Sindbad* the Sailor, in the firft volume, you will think that either the genius of *Homer* was transfufed into the writer, or elfe that he was well acquainted with his works; for he certainly refembles *Homer* in many particulars.—In the boldnefs of his imagination,—in the variety of his characters,—and in the marvellous adventures he relates.—In the hiftory of *Sindbad*, we have moft of thofe that *Ulyffes* meets with

in

in the Odyffey: infomuch that you muft be
convinced the likenefs could not be acci-
dental.

Soph. I can confirm your affertion by my
teftimony,—I have often been furprized at
it.—But *Hortenfius* muft read the ftory in order to be convinced of the refemblance.

Euph. Above all other points the Arabian writer moft refembles *Homer* in his Machinery: with this difference however, that he
is by far the moft modeft in the ufe of it.—
Homer takes the liberty of fending his deities
perpetually on the moft trifling errands,—it
is true the Magicians of the Arabian perform
very marvellous things, by the affiftance of
the good and evil Genii: but then they are
all fubordinate to the feal of the Sultan *Solo-
mon* the fon of *David*,—it is likewife worthy
of obfervation ; that throughout the whole
work, the Supreme Being is never mentioned
without the deepeft marks of homage and
veneration.

Give me leave to mention one more circumftance relating to this work.—That all

C 4   doubts

doubts of its Origin and Authenticity are removed, by the teſtimony of ſeveral writers well acquainted with the original language: particularly by Lady *M. W. Montague*, and by Mr. *Jones*; both of whom bear teſtimony to the fidelity of the Engliſh tranſlation.

Hort. All that you have ſaid, will only prove that this Arabian writer imitated *Homer* as many others have done.

Euph. If I am not miſtaken, it will prove ſomething more;—namely, that there is frequently a ſtriking reſemblance between works of high and low eſtimation, which prejudice only, hinders us from diſcerning, and which when ſeen, we do not care to acknowledge: for the defects of a favourite Author, are like thoſe of a favourite friend; or perhaps ſtill more like our own.

Soph. A palpable hit *Hortenſius !*—confeſs it?

Hort. I confeſs that *Euphraſia* has thrown out many things that have ſurprized, if they have not convinced me, and that I am very deſirous ſhe ſhould proceed.

Soph

Soph. You will then read the Story of *Sind-bad* the Sailor, at our requeſt.

Hort. I will,—but I will not promiſe to al-low the compariſon.

Euph. Not before you are convinced that it is juſt.

Hort. In what claſs will you place your Arabian writer?

Euph. In one of which he is the Origi-nal—Eaſtern Tales:—of which I ſhall ſay more in due time and place. In the mean time, I beg leave to lay down two points as certain; upon which I ſhall eſtabliſh my ſyſtem.

Firſt, That Epic Poetry is the parent of Romance.

Secondly, That there is a certain degree of reſpect due to all the works of Genius, by whatever name diſtinguiſhed.—Grant me theſe two poſtulata, and I ſhall proceed regu-larly.

Hort. I find you will take them for grant-ed.—But I put in a caveat, in objection to your dogmas.

Euph.

Euph. I will call upon you to make them, at a proper time.

Hort. Then I will not interrupt you unseasonably: but perhaps I may sometimes aſk for explanation.

Euph. I will moſt willingly hear and anſwer you, and I beg your aſſiſtance as we go forward.

Soph. It appears to me that *Euphraſia* has advanced nothing that ſhe has not proved, and I expect as ſhe proceeds that ſhe will explain herſelf ſtill further.

Euph. You do me honour,—and I hope juſtice likewiſe.

Hort. Well *Euphraſia,*—I will follow you as cloſely as I can.

Euph. Having traced Romance to its Origin, I ſhall proceed with the progreſs of it: but this ſhall be the ſubject of our next converſation, it is now time to put an end to this.

Soph Let us then adjourn to next Thurſday, at my houſe.

Hort. I will not fail to meet you there.

Soph.

Soph. What would your neighbour *Ergaſtus* ſay, if he ſhould hear that you met weekly two women, to talk of Romances?

Hort. He would certainly indulge his ſplenetic humour at my expence.

Euph. If you are afraid of him, it will be beſt to give over our meetings, for I am meditating to tell the ſubject of them to all the world.

Hort. That is indeed enough to alarm one. I find I muſt take care of what I ſay before you.

Euph. Take courage my friend.—I promiſe you never to make our converſation public, without your conſent and approbation.

Hort. On theſe conditions, I am ſatisfied; I dare ſay you will do nothing raſhly, nor without due conſideration.

Euph. I am honoured by your friendſhip and confidence.—Adieu 'till next Thurſday.

Soph. I ſhall reckon the hours 'till our next meeting.—Adieu!

EVENING

EVENING III.

Hortenſius, Sophronia, Euphraſia.

Hort. WELL met, my fair friends.—
You ſee I am come, although
I hazard the cenſure of *Ergaſtus.*—I proteſt
Euphraſia has carried all her points triumph-
antly.—I ſhall be afraid to attack her in fu-
ture.

Euph. You allow then, I had ſome foundation for my aſſertions.

Hort. I do;—and you have ſtaggered my
opinions in ſome points that I thought im-
moveably fixed and certain:—but much is
yet wanting to make me a perfect convert to
yours.

Euph.

Euph. I shall not entirely rely upon my own strength to effect your conversion, but occasionally call in assistance from abler hands.

Soph. The porch is methinks big enough for the building.—Proceed.

Euph. My dear friend, the building is of greater extent than you imagine, but I will without further prefacing, plunge into the subject. I have traced Romance to an early Origin, and I have mentioned *Homer* as perhaps the first who gave it a regular model or form: I say *perhaps*, because there might be others before him: for doubtless there were Stories transmitted from age to age, before they were committed to writing.

I have seen some Ægyptian stories, of the fabulous kind, that do not fall very short of those in the Mythology of the Greeks and Romans. The Greeks were always fond of these stories.

It is said that one *Dearchus*, a disciple of *Aristotle*, wrote Romances; and he has been called the first writer of them.

Antonius

Antonius Diogenes was the author of a work of this kind, called the Errors and Amours of *Dinias* and *Dercyllis*.

The Amours of *Rhodanis* and *Simonides*, are mentioned as very ancient.

The Romance of *Leucippé* and *Clitophon*, written by *Achilles Tatius*, a Greek, he was afterwards a Bifhop, and his works are ftill extant.

The Ephefian Hiftory by *Xenophon*, might be reckoned in this clafs; alfo the four books of incredible things, written by *Damafius*.— Under the fame clafs may be ranked the fables of *Parthonius Nicenus*,—of *Athenagoras*,— *Theodorus Prodromus*,--*Euftathius*,--and *Longus*,—and many others doubtlefs, whofe names are loft.

Hort. From whence, and to what purpofe have you conjured up fuch a lift of uncouth names—to frighten us?

Euph. Only to fhew you that the Ancients had their Romances, as well as later times,— of thefe works many are loft, and perhaps you would not be much pleafed with thofe that remain.   *Hort.*

Hort. I am a ſtranger to them all, except the Epheſian Hiſtory of *Xenophon.*

Euph. I will be more particular in the next I ſhall mention.—One of the moſt ancient and famous proſe Romances is, The Æthiopic Hiſtory of *Heliodorus,* Biſhop of Tricca in Theſſalia, in the fourth century. It is related, that a Synod conſidering the danger that might happen to youth, from reading a Romance (though there is nothing in it, in the leaſt degree offenſive to morals or modeſty,) authorized by the dignity of its author; propoſed to him either to burn his book, or reſign his Biſhopric, and that he choſe the latter. There are many teſtimonies of the merits of this book, both from ancient, and modern writers; but there needs no other evidence, than the circumſtance of its having been ſucceſſively tranſlated into all the known languages.

Hort. Has it ever been tranſlated into Engliſh.

Euph. Yes certainly, I cannot ſay how early; I do not know of any tranſlation before

fore

fore that of 1687. About the year 1720, there was a new and pompous Edition, published under the second Title of *Theagenes* and *Chariclea*, which I have seen likewise, but I have some reason to believe it was never a popular book here.

Hort. Pray give us your opinion of it?

Euph. It is indisputably a work of Genius, and as such will always be respectable; and moreover, it is one of those Romances that are immediately derived from *Homer.*—The manners of it are evidently imitative of him, and I desire you to respect it on this account.

Hort. Suppose I were disposed to read it, where is it to be found?

Euph. In my own library, at your service. There are doubtless many more of the same kind that are now sunk into oblivion: but this may serve as specimen of the Ancient Romance.

Soph. You are got so far beyond my depth, that I have little to say; but I flatter myself you will come within my reach in due time. I thought myself well read in Romance, but

I

I know nothing of any work you have yet mentioned.

Euph. I shall soon come to your list, but not just at present.—I shall speak first of the Romances of the middle ages; but before I begin I shall read you some extracts from Dr. *Percy,* which will be of great service in our progress through the Regions of Romance.

" That our old Romances of Chivalry
" may be derived in a lineal descent from the
" ancient Historical songs of the Gothic
" bards and scalds will be shown :—and in-
" deed appears the more evident as many
" of these songs are still preserved in the
" North, which exhibit all the seeds of Chi-
" valry before it became a solemn institution.

" Chivalry, as a distinct military order, con-
" ferred in the way of investiture, and ac-
" companied with the solemnity of an oath,
" and other ceremonies, was of later date,
" and sprung out of the feudal constitu-
" tion.—But the ideas of Chivalry prevail-
" ed long before in all the Gothic nation,

VOL. I.   D   and

over

" and may be discovered as in embrio, in the
" customs, manners, and opinions, of every
" branch of that people.——That fondness of
" going in quest of adventures, that spirit of
" challenging to single combat, and that
" respectful complaisance to the fair sex, (so
" different from the manners of the Greeks
" and Romans.), are all of Gothic origin,
" and may be traced up to the earliest times
" among all the Northern nations. These
" existed long before the feudal ages, though
" they were called forth and strengthened in
" a peculiar manner under that constitution,
" and at length arrived at their full maturity
" in the time of the Crusades, so replete with
" Romantic adventures."——This extract
will I hope answer all your doubts and scru-
ples *Hortensius.*

Hort. I confess it confirms your assertions,
and answers your intentions.

Euph, I will tell you my intention,—it si
not to take the honour of making you a convert to myself, but to abler hands.

Hort.

Hort. Then you muſt think me prejudiced indeed.—No Madam, I will owe my con-viction to nobody, if not to you.

Soph. That is handſomely ſaid, and I dare ſay will be made good.—I beg you my dear friend to proceed.

Euph. It is a general received opinion, that the firſt Romances of Chivalry were writ-ten in France.—I think it very doubtful.—I ſuppoſe them to have been current in Spain long before : for the Moors were converſant in them, and many of the old Spaniſh Ro-mances were of Mooriſh derivation ; as ap-pears from the ſtories themſelves.

Soph. I have heard that the name is derived from the French, and it ſeems to me that the Provencals called their works Romaunts.

Euph. That is very true.—Dr. *Percy* will confirm this truth alſo.—" The Latin tongue,
" ceaſed to be ſpoken in France about the ninth
" Century, and was ſucceeded by a mixture
" of the language of the Franks and bad La-
" tin, which was called the Romaunce tongue.
" As the ſongs of Chivalry, became the moſt

D 2   " popular

" popular compositions in that language,
" they were emphatically called Romans,
" Romants, or Romanic, and though this
" name was at first given to either prose,
" or poetry, it came by degrees to be appro-
" priated to prose only, and is now in general
" so used."

Hort. I have long waited to hear the Ety-
mology of this word, and I expected a different derivation of it.

Euph. Will you favour us with your own
sentiments on this head?

Hort. I always thought it was derived
from the Romans, but in what manner I was
ignorant. I conjectured that it arose from an
imitation of their manners.

Euph. I have been desirous to inform myself in this particular, and I give you the best
account I can meet with.—I have read some-
where, that the inhabitants of Normandy,
were formerly called Romandii, or Romandui,
which seems to me the more proper Etymo-
logy.—The French or Franks language came
at length to be called the Romaunt tongue,
as often as the proper name.

Soph.

Soph. I am of the fame opinion, and am told that Romances may be traced in France as high as the eleventh Century.

Euph. Unlefs I am miftaken they may be traced much higher.—I muft read you fome more extracts before I give you a lift of them.

Hort. Your extracts lay heavy upon me. Pray give us your own fentiments and your own obfervations?

Euph. You will have much more reafon to complain when I lay them afide; which I fhall do fhortly, and turn into another road. I fhall make no farther mention of the metrical Romances, than is neceffary to carry us forward to the profe ones.——When they were become popular in France, Spain, Italy, and fome part of Germany, Britain was not unacquainted with them; as witnefs—another extract from Dr. *Percy*—" The ftories " of King Arthur and his round table, may " reafonably be fuppofed to be the growth " of this Ifland. The ftories of *Guy* of War- " wick, and *Bevis* of Southampton, and " others of the fame kind, were probably

D 3   " the

" the invention of the English minstrels.—
" The Welch have some very old Romances
" on the subject of King Arthur, but as
" these are in prose, they are not (probably)
" the first pieces composed on this subject."

Hort. I am extremely glad, for the honour
of *Britain*, that she had early a knowledge of
this polite literature.

Euph. When you thought you were jesting,
you uttered a serious truth; this was indeed
the *polite literature* of those early ages.

These old Historical songs, inspired the enthusiasm of glory, however they may now be
ridiculed.—It is recorded, that at the famous
battle of Hastings, the Normans animated
their courage, by singing the old Romance,
or song of *Rollo.*—Dr. *Percy* says, it was the
song of *Roland*; but the former seems most
likely, because *Rollo* was their ancient chief,
and their Prince traced his descent from him.
—It is indisputable that these songs, had a
strong effect upon the hearers;—but I shall
have occasion to enlarge upon this subject
hereafter. I have said more than I intended

on

on this head, in order to convince *Hortenſius*
of the intimate connexion between the Epic
poetry, and the old Romance.—Pray obſerve,
that I am now ſpeaking of the *O L D* Romance, and not of the imitations of it that
ſprung up many ages afterwards.   They are
frequently confounded together, and from
thence have ariſen the erroneous opinions that
have been formed of them.   I am now ſpeaking of the old Romances of Religion and Chivalry, in which there was a ſtrange mixture of
Paganiſm and Chriſtianity; which was farther
promoted by two Monkiſh writers of thoſe
times; one of which under the fictitious name
of *Turpinus* Archbiſhop of Rheims, wrote a
kind of Hiſtory of *Charlemagne*, and his twelve
peers or Paladins, who drove the Saracens out
of France;—the other our *Geoffery* of Monmouth.   From the firſt of theſe *Arioſto* compoſed, or rather compiled his *Orlando Furioſo*,
and *Taſſo* took the hint of his *Jeruſalem*.—
Dr. *Percy* ſays on this head—" Should the
" public encourage the revival of the an-
" cient ſongs of Chivalry, they would fre-
D 4   quently

" quently fee the rich ore of an *Ariofto* or
" *Taffo*, though buried under the rubbifh and
" drofs of thofe barbarous times."

Hort. I confefs that you have open'd to
me a new vein of learning, which I never before thought worth the trouble of enquiring
after.

Euph. The confeffion is ingenuous.—I ftill
refer you to Dr. *Percy*, though I fhall read no
more extracts from him.

I prefume you are by this time convinced,
that the Romance and Epic poem are nearly
related.—Dr. *Percy* has given us a lift of the
remains of the metrical Romances;—at our
next meeting I will give you mine of profe
ones. For this time I take my leave of you.
I fhall expect you at my houfe next Thurfday.

Hort. & *Sophron.* We will not fail you.

EVENING

EVENING IV.

Sophronia, Hortenfius, Euphrafia.

Hort. I AM impatient to hear the further progrefs of Romance. We have paffed through one department, which has afforded me both information and entertainment, and I expect ftill more from the fucceeding part.

Euph. I am obliged to your candour and attention, and fhall endeavour to merit your indulgence, and the patience with which you have liftened to the dryeft part of our progrefs; I hope we fhall find more entertainment as we go forward.

I fhall now give you my lift of the moft eminent Romances of the *middle ages,* with

as

as many of the dates of the publication, as I
have been able to procure.

I do not pretend to give a regular lift of
them, but only to note fome of the moft celebrated ones, and to mark the diftinction between the *Old Romance*, thofe of the middle
ages, and thofe of the laft divifion neareft our
own times; when the paffion for thefe kind
of writings was revived in France, in the
feventeenth Century. Our own country has
produced many, and as early as any in Europe,
the Spaniards excepted, who received them
from the Moors and Arabians, long before
they were known in France or England.—I
am now fpeaking of the Romances of Chivalry properly fo called.

Geoffery of Monmouth's Hiftory gave
birth to moft of thofe Romances, which are
founded on Englifh ftories.

The Romance of *Hornechild* or King *Horne*,
is one of the oldeft, and is of the metrical
kind.—I know not the date.

Sir *Lancelot du Lake.*

Sir *Guy* of Warwick.

The

The History of King *Arthur* and his Knights of the round table.

Sir *Bevys* of Hampton—*Bevis* of Southampton.

Sir *Degorye.*—Sir *Tristram*—Sir *Perceval.*

All these are extant in metre, and many of them in Prose.

Guy Earl of Warwick, Prose,	1292
Richard Cœur de Lyon, —	1247
Historia Alexandria Regis, —	1245
Destruction of Troy, —	1380

There is good reason to believe that Romances were written in Normandy, long before the time of the Troubadours in Provence.

You will observe that many of the French Romances are founded upon English stories, —for instance,

Le Mort d'Authure, —	1158
Tristan Chevalier de la table Ronde,	1150
Le Brut d'Angleterre, —	1155
Richard Cœur de Lyon, —	1360
Sir Beuves de Hamton,	

Hort. It seems to me that you frequently mention Histories of real persons, among the heroes of Romance.

Euph.

Euph. You are right,—the early Romances were often taken from profe Hiftories; moft of thofe laft mentioned were, and it is worthy your obfervation, that they have been tranflated and tranfcribed from profe to verfe, and *vice verfa*: fo that the fame ftories have appeared, and are ftill extant in both forms.— I will mention a few more French Romances, before I take notice of thofe of Spain.

Hiftoire de Quatre fils d'Aymon,	1156
Le Roman de Rois, ———	1160
Sir Eglamour d'Artois.	
Hiftoire d'Ippomedon.	
Triftan Prince de Lyonnois,	1445
Loves, &c. of the Greek Princes,	1360
Le Chevalier de la Cigne, ——	1435
Roman de Rou.	
Hiftoire de Sangraal.	
Le Romaunt de la Rofe, ———	1409

Hort. I have heard fomething of the laft mentioned, but all the others are ftrangers to to me.

Euph We will fpeak further of it hereafter,—at prefent we will take notice of fome of
the

the most celebrated of the Spanish Romances.

Amadis de Gaul in 24 parts written in the thirteenth Century,

From this famous Romance sprung many imitations. Such as *Amadis* of Greece,—*Palmerin d'Oliva*,—*Palmerin* of England,—*Belianis* of Greece,—and many others, for which I refer you to Don *Quixote*'s library, as we are not likely to meet with them any where else.—I shall only observe that when the art of printing became established in England, most of the old Romances were re-published that had slept many years.—For instance, *Recuyel d'Histoire de Troy*, by *Caxton*, 1470,—*Mort Arthure* by the same,—and many others that I need not mention a second time. There were also some modern Greek Romances,—as *Chæreas & Callirhoe*,—and *Chariton*,—in the 14th Century.

Hort. Upon my word, and a formidable collection! are any of them now extant?

Euph. I believe all, but most of them certainly are.—I will read you an article or two, from a Bookseller's Catalogue, 1777.

Tristan,

Triſtan Chevalier de la table Ronde—belle exemp.—avec figures & vignettes—eleg. rel.— 1548.—Price 1l. 11s. 6d.

Le Romaunt de la Roſe, ou tout l'Art d'A-more et encloſe:—Mſs.—ecrire ſur velin, en lettres Gothique, avec la Capitals illumine, en de plus belle preſervation.—ſur le dernier fuillé eſt cette remarque. " *Johan Anquetin,* " *Bailif, a preſent Count de Harcourt, fait* " *deviſé et ecrire cette Romaunt de la Roſe,* " *par Johan Selles, Clerc.*"—*Accomplir en l'Ann de Incarnation,* 1409—Price 1l. 11s. 6d.

Hort. Very curious indeed,—and the price ſhews its eſtimation.

Euph. Another Edition of the ſame work *printed* —— —— 1541
　　　　Another, at Amſterdam,　1735

Soph. I have heard much of the Romance of the Roſe, and I wiſh to know more parti-culars of it.

Hort. Euphraſia ſmiles, I fancy ſhe could give us ſome.

Euph. I believe I can but it will interrupt our progreſs; when I have finiſhed my liſt, I will tell you all that I know of it.

Soph.

Soph. You cannot oblige us more.

Euph. I find myself obliged to mention many of these works, which were of early invention; according to the date of their *translation*;—as, *Romaunt de la Chevalieres de Gloire,*—Paris, 1612.—The Caftell of Love, a Spanish Romance.—Translated into English by *John Bourchier* (Lord *Berners*); who also translated many other Romances from the French, Spanish, and Italian, particularly, The History of the noble and valyant Knight, Sir *Arthur* of Lytell Britain, (Armorica).— The famous exploits of Sir *Hugh* of Bourdeaux.—This nobleman died in the year 1532.

Soph. A proof that Romances were early known here:—but you seem to have finished your lift.

Euph. I underftand you, and will now fulfil my promise.—The Romance of the Rose, is, properly fpeaking, a courfe of Love-philofophy,—it was begun by *William de Lorris,* who undertook it to pleafe a Lady with whom he was enamour'd,—he died in 1260, leaving it unfinished.—Forty years after; one *John de Meun*

Meun, who was alſo called *le Clopinell*, wrote a continuation of it; he was a Dominican, and a Doctor of Divinity.

Soph. He was not like the Greek Biſhop, ordered to burn his work?

Euph. Times and manners were changed; Prieſts wrote Romances, and Princes read them.—This *John de Meun* dedicated another Romance of his, to King *Philip le Bel*, in which he mentions his former work, as a recommendation of his new one.

" I *John de Meun*, who formerly upon jea- " louſy, putting *Belacoil* into priſon, taught " how to take the Caſtell, and gather the " Roſe, &c."—Many of the French writers extol this Romance very highly, and prefer it to all the works of the Italian Poets; but it is cuſtomary with them, to depreciate the writers of other countries, and to magnify their own. As another proof of the affinity of metrical and proſe Romances, this famous one was tranſlated into Proſe, in the year 1480, by *Johan de Moulinet*, who is ſaid to have enriched it with many Allegories of his

own

own invention. It afterwards underwent several further alterations, from the different hands it paſſed through; but ſtill the ground work was the ſame, and it ſtill preſerved its eſtimation.

Hort. Pray was it ever tranſlated into Engliſh?

Euph. It was begun by *Chaucer*, but left unfiniſhed at his death. I can give you a ſpecimen of this work, if you wiſh to hear it.

Soph. By all means:—Let us hear it?

Extract *from* CHAUCER.

Menne ſaine that in ſwevenings†,
There nis but fables and leſings,
But menne may know, ſome ſwevens ſent,
And afterwards been appaurent;
This I ſhall draw unto warraunt.

Within my twenty year of age
When that love taketh his courage
Of youngé folke, I wente ſoone
To bedde as I was wonte to doone,
And faſt I ſlepte, and in ſleeping
Me mette with ſuch a ſwevening,
That liked me wondrous wele,
And in this ſweven is never a dele,

† Dreams.

That

That it nis afterwards befal,
Like as this dreme will tell us all.

Now this dreme will I rhime aright
To make your herts both gay and light,
For Love he praieth, and alſo
Commaundeth me that it be ſo.

Now if there be any aſke of me
Whether it be he or ſhe,
How this book that I read you here
Shall hight? that I will now declare.
It is THE ROMAUNT OF THE ROSE,
In which all the art of Love I cloſe.

The matter fair is of to make,
God graunt me in greé that ſhe it take
For whom that in begonnen is,
And that is ſhe that hath I wis
Such mokell priſe, and thereto ſhe
So worthy is beloved to be,
That ſhe well ought of priſe and right,
Be 'cleped Roſe of every wight.

Euph. I reckon that by this time, I have tired you ſufficiently.

Soph. Not me I am ſure, you have ſatisfied my curioſity.

Hort. Nor me.—I find this account both curious and entertaining, and we are obliged for the communication.

Euph.

Euph. I hope by this time *Hortenſius* is convinced, that Romances, have been written, both in proſe and verſe; and further that a Romance, is nothing but an Epic in proſe.

Hort. I give up the point,—but I reſerve the liberty of making the proper diſtinction between the claſſic Poets, and Romance writers.

Euph. We will ſpeak further on that head hereafter,—at preſent, I have ſtill a more arduous undertaking to ſupport, namely, that theſe writings were by no means ſo contemptible, as they have been repreſented by later writers:—by thoſe who never ſaw them, nor knew any particulars of them; but have condemned them indiſcriminately, through blind prejudice; or what is worſe, total ignorance of them.

Hort. I take ſhame to myſelf, and ſhall remain ſilent on this head.

Euph. In early times, in the dawning of literature, theſe ſubjects exerciſed the pens of the ingenious—they were the favourite ſtudies of the young nobility and gentry of thoſe

times

times, and their manners were, in a great
meafure formed upon the models of thofe
adventurers, whofe exploits they continually
heard recited.   The effects they produced
were indeed of fo mixed a nature, that it is
difficult to feparate the good from the bad.
Religion and virtue, were fo blended with fanaticifm and abfurdity, that the luftre of the
former principles, concealed the blemifhes of
the latter.——At this diftance of time we need
not be afraid to give our judgment of
them, neither ought we to be afhamed to do
juftice to works of Genius, by whatever
name they are called.

Hort. Certainly.——I fhall pay them due
refpect for your fake.

Euph. Not fo, *Hortenfius*, I will not accept fuch refpect for them.——You fhall pay it
for the fake of thofe illuftrious men, who imbibed their enthufiafm, and carried it into
practice.

Thefe were the books that caufed fuch a
fpirit of Chivalry in the youth of much later
times, particularly in Spain; fuch as raifed

up

up a *Cervantes* to attack them; and you will find a curious lift of them, in the fixth chapter of the firft book of Don *Quixote*, in the converfation between the Prieft and the Barber; in which the Author condemns moft of them to the flames.

Hort. Is it poffible to refpect that incomparable work, and yet refpect the books it condemns and ridicules?

Euph. Yes it is; though it may feem at firft view a paradox.—This infatuation was was fo general, that the brighteft geniufes, and the wifeft men were not exempt from it. —Our Poetry owes more to it, than you imagine; it was calculated to elevate and warm a poetic imagination, of this I fhall bring proofs. *Chaucer*, and all our old writers, abound with it,—*Spencer* owes perhaps his immortality to it, it is the Gothic imagery, that gives the principal graces to his work, and without them we fhould foon grow tired of his Allegories,—but we have a yet ftronger inftance in our divine *Milton*, whofe mind was fo deeply impreffed by them, and his imagination fo

E 3   warmed

warmed, that he frequently recurs to them, of which I shall only give you a few specimens.——

> Fairer than feigned of old, or fabled since
> Of Fairy damsels met in foreft wide
> By knights of Logres, or of Lyones,
> *Lancelot,* or *Pelleas,* or *Pellenore.* PAR. REG. b. 2.

And again in the following book.——

> When *Agrican* with all his northern powers
> Befieged *Albracca, as Romances tell,*
> The city of Galliphrone;——from thence to win
> The faireft of her fex *Angelica*
> His daughter; fought by many proweft knights,
> Both *Paynim,* and the peers of *Charlemagne.*

There are continual allufions of this kind, fprinkled through all his works; but thefe may ferve as proofs of what I have advanced.

Hort. You find means to authenticate what ever you advance.

Soph. Give me leave to furnish you with another paffage, from memory, it is in the Penferofo.——

> Or call up him that left half told
> The ftory of *Cambufcan* bold,
> Of *Camball,* and of *Algarfife,*
> And who who had *Canacé* to wife,

That

That own'd the virtuous ring and glaſs;—
And of the wondrous horſe of braſs
On which the Tartar king did ride:—
And if ought elſe great bards beſide
In ſage and ſolemn tunes have ſung
Of turneys and of trophies hung,
Of foreſts and enchantments drear
Where more is meant than meets the ear.

Euph. I am much obliged to you, this paſſage helps to illuſtrate our ſubjeſt.—I will
only juſt obſerve that the ſtory *of Canacé* is
finiſhed by *Spencer* in the Fairy Queen, Book
4th, where he begins the ſtory with a fine
Apoſtrophe to *Chaucer's* memory.

Hort. There is a kind of enthuſiaſm, that
is inſpired by theſe Poets, which ſeizes the
head, and engages the heart, in their favour.
—I have heard it obſerved that *Spencer* has
made more poets than any other writer of
our country.

Soph. I know one inſtance of it myſelf, in
a lady, who never before dreamed of writing
Poetry, ſhe was not young at the time when
ſhe firſt met with *Spencer*; and reading ſome
of the fineſt Cantos in it, the impreſſion was

E 4 ſo

so strong, that she could not sleep all the night after, and before the morning, she composed a very pretty piece of Poetry in honour of *Spencer*.—and from that time forward, she continued to write whenever a subject fell in her way, and all her writings are above mediocrity.

Euph. I can confirm this truth, and that she wrote verses when she was turned of seventy years of age.

Hort. My dear Ladies, you are enough to frighten one, I shall be afraid to take up one of these books, lest it should work such a miracle upon me.:—but are we not wandering from our subject?

Soph. I beg your pardon, it is I that have led you astray.

Euph. Not so far as *Hortensius* seems to think, for *Spencer*'s poem may be called of the Romance kind.—He will allow that there must have been something engaging and fascinating in those books that captivated the hearts of men, who were in other respects of sound minds and regular conduct:—for ought

we

we to think that all who read and admired those books were fools or madmen?

Hort. According to your account, we must reckon all the most accomplished men of those times in the number if we do.

Euph. In the days of Gothic ignorance, these Romances might perhaps, be read by many young persons as true Histories, and might therefore more easily affect their manners.—As in the Heathen Mythology, the example of a mortal exalted into a demi-god, was an incitement to the imitation of actions so gloriously rewarded;—so the examples of the Heroes of Romance and Epic poetry, might have excited the youth of those times, to copy exploits universally rewarded by praise and admiration.

Hort. It is neither incredible, nor improbable that they might do so; and you have well explained the Paradox, I took notice of.

Euph. This infatuation spread through France, Italy, Germany, and England; but more remarkably in Spain, where the young nobility were so deeply infected by it, that it

called

called forth the pen of a *Cervantes*; who by ridiculing Romance and Knight Errantry in his Don *Quixote*, in some degree checked this frenzy: but the effect of his ridicule was not so universal as is generally believed.

Hort. Are you going to maintain another Paradox?

Euph. Not at all—I am only speaking a well known truth, and I shall only appeal to Dr. *Percy.*—" The Satire of *Cervantes*, or, " *rather* the increase of knowledge and " literature, drove these books off the stage."

Hort. Now you are coming upon us, with your extracts again.

Euph. Not so.—I shall endeavour for once to stand my ground alone.—The passion for these books was in some degree checked; but it was not eradicated.—There is good reason to believe, that even *Cervantes* himself, was not cured of it.

Hort. Nay, if you animadvert upon *Cervantes*, I know not what to say :—but I shall expect proofs of this assertion.

Euph. I shall produce them presently.—

Besides

Besides his *Galatea*; (of which he speaks with pleasure, and rescues it from the condemned books in Don *Quixote*'s library, and after he had written his Novels upon a new plan,) he composed a serious Romance, called *Persiles* and *Sigismonda*, which remains extant, as a proof against him. It is said that he preferred this to all his other works:—he compares it with the Æthiopics of *Heliodorus*, being written in the same style and manner. What shall we say of the man, who had produced Don *Quixote*, and could afterwards write a book of the same kind as those he satyrized? May we not conclude that he still loved them in his heart?

Hort. Permit me to offer a reason on his behalf,—a reason that makes me sigh over the fate of Genius.—*Cervantes!* the gallant soldier!—the delightful companion!—the charming writer!—the pride and boast of his country!—*Cervantes* wanted bread.—he wrote this celebrated work in a prison, and knowing the taste and humour of his countrymen, composed such a book, as was most likely to please them, and procure relief to his miseries.

Euph

Euph. Your apology is generous and liberal, and you have given us, probably, the true
reaſon.—I join with you, in admiring and de-
ploring the fate of that incomparable man, and
in him, of neglected Genius.—I am now going, as you will think, to maintain another
Paradox; to affirm that the paſſion for the
Old Romance, ſtill exiſts in ſome countries:
—particularly, in Spain and Italy.

Hort. How will you bring proofs of this
point?

Euph. By appealing to the veracity of our
friend *Horatio*, whom you knew a man to
be believed. *Horatio* reſided twenty years
in Italy, and was a cloſe obſerver of the manners of the place where he reſided.—He told
me that in the city of Naples, (and many
other places) there are a ſet of people who
earn their bread by reciting old ſtories, that
they are ſurrounded by a ſet of auditors who
give them ſmall money.—They put one in
mind of the old bards, except that they recite ſometimes in proſe, as well as in verſe,—
they recite in a kind of tone between ſpeaking

ing and singing, something like the Opera recitative,—they are frequently sent for to attend the sick, whom they lull to sleep by their chantings,—sometimes they recite from their invention, but oftener from their memory,—sometimes stanzas of *Ariosto* and *Tasso*;—sometimes from the old Romances;—at others the legendary stories of the saints of the Romish church, but they are much followed, and most people are pleased with their recitals, and they are very popular.

Soph. I have heard that there are still itinerant bards in Italy and Spain.

Euph. You are not misinformed. *Horatio* has heard two of them contend in alternate verse, and with all the warmth and enthusiasm of the ancient Poets.—Neither the spirit of Poetry or Romance, is totally extinct, in many parts of Italy and Spain.

Hort. Whenever I think to catch you tripping, you glide away from me, and in your place I find another person, whom I am to contend with.

Euph. I only fortify my opinions, by others more respectable.

Hort.

Hort. You fight flying like a Parthian, but I will confefs freely that you have given me a much higher opinion of thefe old Romances, and of thofe who read them. But what then are thofe of which I had formed fo contemptible an opinion ?

Euph. Ah *Hortenfius!*—have I not caught you tripping ?—Have you fuffered yourfelf to form a contemptible opinion of books you never knew, nor enquired after?

Hort. If I have taken up an opinion upon truft, it was from the character that has been given me of thofe books, by perfons of acknowledged abilities and judgment.

Euph. Then do not part with it till you fee good reafon for it, perhaps your friends may have given you a true reprefentation: there are many paltry Romances, and but few capital ones.—But I fhall come nearer to you at our next meeting, when I am to fpeak of yet a third clafs, which I fhall call *modern Romances*, and indeed they are fo comparatively; I mean thofe of the fixteenth and feventeenth Centuries, we will now take our leave of the *OLD* Romances.

Hort.

Hort. Thus far you have gone forward succefsfully, and I am much obliged for your communications.

Euph. And I to you for your patience, which I fhall put to further trial.

Soph. Pray banifh that Idea, left it fhould lead you to fupprefs or abridge any thing.— Next Thurfday we meet at my houfe.

Hort. I fhall attend you with increafed fatisfaction.

Euph. Good night to my kind and partial friends.

EVENING

EVENING V.

Hortensius, Sophronia, Euphrasia.

Euph. WE are now to proceed to the modern Romances, which have been so often mistaken for the old ones.— after these had been exploded in a great measure, the taste for them was revived in France, by *Calprenede,*—*D'Urfé,*—the *Scudery*'s, and many others; who wrote new Romances upon a different plan: which in some kinds of refinement were superior to the old ones, but in the greater merits fell very short of them. They were written with more regularity, and brought nearer to probability; but on the other hand by taking for their foundation some obscure parts of true history, and building

ing

ing fictitious stories upon them, truth and fiction were so blended together, that a common reader could not distinguish them, young people especially imbibed such absurd ideas of historical facts and persons, as were very difficult to be rectified.—Why does *Sophronia* smile at my remark?

Soph. Because it reminds me of a circumstance, that confirms the truth of your observation.—A sister of mine was upon a visit in the country.—She slept with a lady who was a visitor at the same house.—The room was hung with fine old Tapestry, representing the history of *Alexander* the Great.—The stranger lady asked the story, and my sister pointed out the tent of *Darius* as the capital piece.—Pray said the stranger, which of those ladies is *Cassandra?*—my sister was surprized and at a loss for an answer.—I don't know said she, that any person of that name is there.—Oh, said the lady, I mean *Statira*; she is sometimes called by that name, and sometimes by the other.—My sister was confounded to discover how ignorant she was of *Statira*'s history, and

said

said no more.—At her return home she told me of this incident, I was at no loss to understand it.—I told her that *Statira* many Centuries after her death, had been revived by a certain French writer, and made the subject of a long Romance, under the name of *Cassandra*.

Euph. Your story illustrates my observation, and proves the impropriety of putting these books into the hands of young people, though in other respects they are a very harmless kind of reading.

Soph. I have heard that these books produced a particular kind of affectation in speaking and writing, which is still called the Romantic.

Euph. That is very probable,—but as fashion has too great a share in regulating the language of the times, that could not last very long.

Soph. I beg your pardon.—Fashion did not then change so often as now.

Euph. I believe there has always been nearly the same proportion of fashionable folly in civilized countries; the only difference

ence is, that within the prefent Century it has made a much quicker rotation. To trace the caufes of this would lead us too far from our prefent fubject.—When people talk in an affected manner, and ftill more when they utter improbabilities, it may without impropriety be called Romantic, at any time.

Hort. You, ladies, may fettle this point at any other time.—I beg you, Madam, to proceed to your modern Romances.

Euph. The ancient and modern Romance, had each their peculiar *ton*, their *affectation*, their *abfurdities:*—at the fame time it muft be confeffed by thofe who defpife them, that the enthufiafm they infpired was that of virtue and honour.

Soph. That is indifputable.—I have read many of thefe you are now fpeaking of, and I can bear my teftimony that they inculcated no principles contrary to any of the moral or focial virtues.

Euph. You fay true.—If it taught young women to deport themfelves too much like Queens and Princeffes, it taught them at the

F 2   fame

same time that virtue only could give lustre to every rank and degree.—It taught the young men to look upon themselves as the champions and protectors of the weaker sex;—to treat the object of their passion with the utmost respect;—to avoid all improper familiarities, and, in short, to expect from her the reward of their virtues.

Hort. Upon my word, ladies, you have said more in behalf of these books, than you have against them; and with every appearance of reason.

Euph. I am glad you think so, and begin to hope we shall agree in opinion still better, as we advance farther.

Such as I have described them, are the French Romances.—The *Astrea* of *D'Urfé*,—*Cyrus* and *Clelia* by *Mesdemoiselles Scudery*,—*Cassandra* and *Cleopatra* by *Calprenede*,—*Ariane*,—*Almahide*,—*Polexander*, —*Ibrahim*, —*Francion*,—and many others of the same kind.—These were the books that pleased our grandmothers, whose patience in wading thro' such tremendous volumes, may raise our surprize:

prize: for to us they appear dull,—heavy,—and uninteresting.

Soph. You remind me of what my good Aunts have often told me, that they, my Mother, and a select party of relations and friends, used to meet once a week at each others houses, to hear these stories;—one used to read, while the rest ply'd their needles.

Hort. Such an assembly would excite a smile in the ladies of this enlightened age, who know how to employ their time so much better.

Soph. Spare your reflections *Hortensius.*—I presume to think these meetings were quite as innocent, though perhaps in some respects not so *improving*, as the *Coteries,* and *Card-assemblies* of our days.

Euph. I am entirely of your opinion, my friend: and I believe *Hortensius* meant a reflection upon the present age, rather than the past.

Hort. I presume not to decide a point of so much consequence.—The Ladies of the present age, have the advantages of a more

liberal

liberal education, whether they make a better use of them, depends on themselves.

Euph. I believe they have not the patience of their ancestors, in reading such tedious stories, and that most of them would submit to any penance to avoid it.   These books are now become the lumber of a bookseller's shop, and are frequently seen to wrap a pound of sugar from the grocer's.   I have dip'd into them, in order to qualify myself to speak of their merits and defects; and I declare that nothing but a prison, and no other companion, could induce me to read one of them through.

Hort. Are not these the books that I have heard despised so much?

Euph. I believe they are:—yet among loads of trash, we may select some works of Genius, that deserve to be celebrated, and transmitted to posterity.

————" that which we call a Rose,
By any other name would smell as sweet."   SHAKESP.

I ask your permission to read another short extract from Dr. *Percy?*

Hort.

Hort. Your humble servant Madam,—
pray read what you please."

Euph. " The first prose Romances that
" appeared in our language were printed by
" *Caxton*, (at least that I have been able to dis-
" cover,) and these were translations from
" the French:—Whereas Romances had long
" been current in metre, and read in *Chau-
" cer*'s time."

Hort. They shall be prose or verse, for any
opposition from me.

Euph. In the beginning of Queen *Elizabeth*'s reign these books began to be much
read, and towards the end of it, Romances
were written in our language.—One of the
earliest and most famous that I know of, is
Euphues, or the Anatomy of Wit, by *John
Lilly*, who attempted to reform and purify
the English language, by purging it of obso-
lete and uncouth expressions. Mr. *Blount*
who published *Lilly*'s plays, speaks of this
work in his Preface. " Our nation is obliged
" to *Lilly* for a new kind of English which
" he taught it,—all our ladies were his

F 4. " scholars,

" scholars; and that beauty at Court that
" could not *parléz Euphuisme*;—that could
" not converse in his language,—was as lit-
" tle regarded as she who now speaks not
" French."

Other writers speak very differently of this
work. One calls it an affected Jargon, in
which the perpetual use of metaphors, allu-
sions and allegories, pass for wit, and stiff
bombast for fine language; that the court of
Elizabeth was miserably infected by it, which
helped to let in the vile pedantry that was predominant in the following reign. This diver-
sity of opinions induced me to purchase the
book, which by good fortune, I met with
soon after.

Hort. You will then give us your own opinion of it?

Euph. I esteem it as a great curiosity.—The
language exceeded my expectation, but there
is a certain quaintness and peculiarity, that
would not be borne with at this time; yet we
should always consider it as written in the
dawning of our language, and as a step to the
improvement of it, which soon after shone out
with

with great luftre under *Shakefpear*, *Fletcher*, and *Johnfon*.

Hort. I fhould like to fee this book.

Euph. I am afraid you are not a fufficient adept in Romance, to have any relifh for it. —It is printed in the black letter—" The " firft part is called *Euphues* or the Anato- " my of Wit.—Very pleafant for all Gen- " tlemen to reade, and moft neceffary to re- " member; wherein is contained the delights " that Wit followeth in his Youth, by the " pleafantnefs of Love, and the happineffe he " reapeth in age, by the perfectneffe of Wif- " dom.—Printed 1620.

" The fecond Part is entitled *Euphues* and " his England, containing his Voyage and " Adventures.—Printed in 1623, and Dedi- " cated to *Edward Vere*, Earl of Oxenford, " Great Chamberlain of England."

Soph. I fhall not be fatisfied with this ac- count.—I muft read it.

Euph. Whenever you pleafe.—The next work of this kind I fhall mention is, *Parthe- niffa*, a Romance, by *Roger Boyle*, Earl of

Orrery,

Orrery,—in three Volume folio, Printed 1664.

Hort. Mercy on us!—three Volumes in Folio!

Euph. Yea, and here follows a remark upon it, by Mr. *Walpole,* from his Royal and noble Authors.——

" The Earl's Biographer fays, that this per-
" formance has not been much read, becaufe
" it never was compleated; as if three Vo-
" lumes in Folio wou'd not content the moft
" heroic appetite that ever exifted."

Hort. Truly I am of his opinion. I fuppofe it was the fafhion both to write, and to read thefe voluminous works, at that time.

Euph. I believe it was.—That eternal fcribler the Duchefs of Newcaftle wrote many ftories of the fame kind, which were publifhed in 1665, in one volume folio, called—*Nature's Pictures drawn by Fancy to the Life.*

Hort. Thank heaven, it is not the fafhion to read fuch long works now!

Euph. You may always throw afide your book, when you are tired. The wits of thefe days have more fqueamifh appetites, and the

writers

writers of both times studied the taste of their readers.

Let us return to our subject.—The next work of merit I shall mention, is Sir *Philip Sidney*'s Arcadia, which has been highly celebrated, by his contemporaries; and indeed by many later writers. This Romance is of a mixed kind, partaking of the heroic manners of the old Romance, and the simplicity of pastoral life.

Hort. This book has been excepted from the general censure passed upon others of the same class. The Author was reckoned one of the first characters of his age,—or rather the Phœnix of it.

Euph. After what you have said, I shall not attempt the character of this celebrated work:—but I will read you an extract from Mr. *Walpole*'s catalogue of Royal and Noble Authors.——

" No man seems to me so astonishing an
" object of temporary admiration as Sir *Phi-*
" *lip Sidney*. The learned of Europe dedi-
" cated their works to him, the republic of
" Poland thought him worthy to be in no-
                                    " mination

" mination for their crown.—All the Mufes
" of England wept for his death.—When we
" at this diftance enquire what prodigious
" merits excited fuch admiration,—what do
" do we find?—Great valour.—But it was an
" age of heroes. In full of all other talents,
" we have a tedious, lamentable, pedantic,
" Paftoral romance, which the patience of a
" young virgin in love, cannot now wade
" through: and fome abfurd attempts to
" fetter Englifh verfe in Roman chains; a
" proof that this applauded author under-
" ftood little of the genius of his own lan-
" guage.—The few of his letters extant are
" poor matters.—By far the beft prefumption
" of his abilities as a writer, is a pamphlet,
" which is an anfwer to *Leicefter*'s Common-
" wealth.—It defends his uncle with great
" fpirit:—he died with the rafhnefs of a vo-
" lunteer, after having lived to write with
" the *fang froid*, and prolixity of *Mademoi-*
" *felle de Scuderi.*

Hort. I think the character of Sir *Philip
Sidney*, too much degraded here.

                                             Euph.

Euph. In justice to the writer, I must give you the note that follows.——

" I have been blamed (says Mr. *Walpole*,) " for not mentioning Sir *Philip*'s defence of " poetry, which some think his best work,— " all that my criticisms pretended to say, was, " that I could not conceive how a man who " in some respects had written dully and weak- " ly, and who at best was far inferior to our " best Authors, had obtained such immense " reputation.—Let his merits, and his fame " be weighed together, and then let it be de- " termined whether the world has overvalu- " ed, or I have undervalued the character of " Sir *Philip Sidney*."

Hort. Truly I think he has undervalued it. His credit as a writer, out of the question; there will remain qualities enough, to justify the respect paid to Sir *Philip*, by his contemporaries.

Euph. You will recollect that his merits as a *writer*, was the point that fell under Mr. *Walpole*'s consideration, and also that it is a *man* who is the author of this critique.

Hort.

Hort. I underſtand you:—but has a *woman* nothing to ſay in defence of a work that has always been a favourite with her ſex?

Euph. Our ſex are certainly obliged to Sir *Philip*, who paid us great deference upon all occaſions. The Arcadia is addreſſed to his accompliſhed ſiſter the Counteſs of Pembroke, and is commonly called, Pembroke's Arcadia.

Hort. Still you are ſilent as to the merits of it.

Euph. Since you will oblige me to ſpeak out, I think it equal, but not ſuperior to any of the Romances of the ſame period. The proſe part of it, is much ſuperior to the poetry; as will appear by comparing it with that of his contemporaries. *Spenſer*'s Shepherd's Calender is ſtill intelligible, and pleaſant: but *Sidney*'s Paſtorals, are dull and unintelligible, and are generally ſkipped over by thoſe who ſtill read and admire the Arcadia.

Soph. I confeſs that is exactly the caſe with me, who ſtill have the courage to declare I think it a very fine Romance.

Soph.

Euph. So do many others, and I do not see any reason why people should be ashamed to avow their taste.—I have a few words more to add on this subject.—Sir *Philip Sidney* died in 1586. The date of my edition of the Arcadia is 1627:—but I should suppose there must have been an earlier one.—In 1725, it underwent a kind of Translation by Mrs. *Stanley*, by which it was thought to lose more beauties than it gained.—It is now time for us to leave his works to their repose, upon the shelves of the learned, and the curious in old writings.

Soph. I shall come and awaken the Arcadia, in order to refresh my memory. I lov'd this book in my youth, and shall not forsake it now.

Euph. My friend, what you say is one of the strongest objections to books of this class. If read and liked early in life, they are apt to give a romantic turn to the reader's mind, unless she has as much discretion as *Sophronia*.

Soph. I do not deserve the compliment,—I had really the turn of mind you mention, till a little knowledge of the world, and my

experience

experience in it, corrected the abfurd ideas I had conceived.

Euph. You are very ingenuous, and your confeſſion confirms my opinion.—The next work I ſhall introduce to you, is *Barclay's Argenis,* which you already know to be a favorite of mine.—It is doing it an injury to treat it as a mere Romance ; for the ſtory is only a vehicle to convey to us, the genius and knowledge of the Author. A writer of the laſt Century thus ſpeaks of it.——

" The philoſophy and politics of *Barclay's* " *Argenis,* have made it worthy of the peru- " ſal of the greateſt ſtateſmen and ſcholars."

The name of Romance, even in our days, had prejudiced many people againſt it—you among the reſt *Hortenſius.*

Hort. I confeſs it. I thought you had employed your time to little purpoſe in reviving an old Romance; but on reading it, I was convinced that it was a work of real merit, and deſerved a better reception.

Euph. There are ſome Critics among us, that ought to have informed themſelves better,

ter, before they prefumed to impofe their opinions upon the public, which they have mifinformed, and put it out of their power to rectify the erroneous opinions they have occafioned.

Hort. The Reviewers I prefume.—I remember there was fomething faid, that I thought ill-natured, but I do not recollect the particulars.

Euph. I have in my hand an extract from the Critical Review of January 1772,——
" Notwithftanding the pains taken in an Ad-
" vertifement to put off this Phœnix, for an
" Original work, we will venture to pro-
" nounce it a tranflation of the *Argenis* of
" *Barclay.*—That a Lady may have given
" us a tranflation of that compofition is not
" impoffible; but we rather imagine that an
" old tranflation has been modernifed.—The
" *Argenis* has been highly commended by fe-
" veral learned and ingenious men, but we
" own ourfelves to have no relifh for the
" Romances of the laft Century, we are fuffici-
" ently fatisfied with thofe of the prefent."—
What think you of this fentence?

Hort. Arbitrary and decisive; with an air of neglect and contempt, that is calculated to prejudice the public against it:—but pray had this mandate any effect upon the sale of your publication?

Euph. Too much so, on the public in general:—but I have a circle of friends who cannot be biassed by these self elected censors of books.—If these doughty Critics, had read the *Preface only*, they would have been satisfied, that neither the *Editor*, nor the *Publisher*, ever intended *to put off this Phœnix for an original work*; though by its being advertised with some other original publications, it gave a pretence to those who look no farther than *advertisements*, to put so unfair a construction on it.

Hort. Very unfair dealing indeed.

Euph. These sagacious inquisitors *ventured to pronounce* it the *Argenis* of *Barclay*,—amazing penetration, and equal discretion!—had they afforded so much of their precious time, as was necessary to read the *Preface* only, they would have known that the Editor
                                   was

was so far from desiring to disguise or conceal the truth, that she took pleasure and pride in acknowledging it and, in short they would have met with a full confutation of every point they advanced against her.

Soph. Their sentence was both cruel and unjust, but I hope it recoiled upon themselves.

Hort. It seems to me that they looked no farther than the Title-page, and gave their sentence, by guessing at the contents of the book.

Euph. I have every reason to believe so :— but peace be to them and their labours, which if they were not well paid for, they would soon discontinue.—It is not in their power to add to, or take away from the reputation of *Barclay*'s *Argenis*, whatever it may have gained or lost by any of its translators or commentators.

Hort. But how did you come off from the rest of the Inquisitors?

Euph. The Monthly Reviewers were more liberal and candid,—they read the *Preface*, nay they commended it, and paid due respect

G 2   to

to the Original writer: but they objected to the politics, as local and temporary; and to the principles of government, as absolute and arbitrary.—They took no notice that the high monarchical principles of *Barclay* were moderated by the Editor. I could also have wished them to have cast an eye upon the Poetry, which is no inconsiderable part of the work, nor, as I hope, the worst executed. I confess I was mortified to find they did not; for though I expected they would find something to correct, I hoped they would likewise find something to commend.—But I have said too much upon this subject, and shall conclude with observing, it was the best book I ever gave the public, and the worst received.

Hort. It is indisputably a work of great merit:—but pray allow me to ask a question, —how came you to alter the Original title, and call it the Phœnix?

Euph. It was against my own judgment and remonstrance.—The Publisher advised, and even insisted upon a *new Title*, and I the rather

ther

ther gave way to his demand, becauſe there
was another Tranſlation offer'd to the preſs,
and intended to be publiſhed at the ſame
time; and I thought my friends would know
mine by this diſtinction:—this was the private
reaſon hinted at in the Preface, which was ridiculed by the Reviewers.

Soph. I have heard that your Tranſlation
is conſiderably abridged.

Euph. It is ſo,—I wiſh it had been abridged as much more, and that I had only told
the plain narrative, and omitted all the fine
Eſſays, (the moſt valuable part of the work,)
and the poetry alſo; it had ſaved me much
time and labour, and would have pleaſed
more readers.

Hort. But not ſuch readers, as *you* wiſh to
pleaſe.

Euph. Thoſe are the beſt readers for an Author that buy the moſt books, but enough of
this.   I muſt obſerve that *J. Barclay* was of
Scotiſh parentage, but born and educated in
France, and that he was an accompliſhed gentleman. Thoſe who deſire to know more of him,
muſt read his works;—which are, The *Argenis*,

G 3   and

and *Euphormio*, a fatyrical work.   You are
now I truft convinced of the affinity of
Profe, and metrical Romances.

Chaucer's Canterbury tales would tell equally well in verfe or profe.   His Knight's tale is
a complete Epic, and in *Dryden*'s opinion very little inferior to the Iliad or the Æneis.—
" The ftory (fays he) is more pleafing, the
" manners as perfect, the diction as poetical,
" the learning as deep and various, and the
" conduct as artful."   Permit me to remark
that *Dryden*'s elegant, rich, and harmonious
numbers, have preferved this, and many other
of *Chaucer*'s works, from finking into oblivion, and he has given the old Bard a fhare
of his own immortality.

Spenfer's Faery Queen, is confeffedly a Romance verfified.

Fenelon's *Telemachus*, is an Epic in profe.
—The *Telemachus* is a work above all praife,
and demands our notice here, as being a ftory
of the Heroic kind.

Ramfey's *Cyrus* is an excellent work, but it
has more of the caft of Hiftory than of Romance

mance. I mention both thefe charming
books rather out of time, becaufe they are
of a different fpecies, from the modern ftories or Novels.

Hort. And of more value than a million of
them, though you have fpoken fo very briefly
of them.

Euph. To praife them is to hold a candle to the Sun.

I fhall now draw towards a conclufion of
Romances properly fo called.—I fhall read
you an extract, which is the conclufion of the
converfation of the Canon and the Curate in
the fourth book of Don *Quixote*; in the
courfe of which, all the abfurdities of Romances have been expofed and criticifed.—
" The fubject of a Romance (fays the Ca-
" non) affords an ample field for a good Ge-
" nius to difplay itfelf.—He may weave a
" web of fuch various aud beautiful texture,
" that the perfection of it may attain to
" the ultimate end of all writing, which is to
" delight ahd inftruct mankind; becaufe
" this unconfined way of writing, gives an
" Author room to fhew his fkill, in the Epic

G 4 or

" or the Lyric way, in Tragedy or Comedy;
" with all the parts included in the sweet and
" charming sciences of Poetry and Oratory:"
—for the Epic may be written in *prose*, as
well as *verse*,

Hort. You end, as you always do, with a
clincher to your argument.

Euph. Let us then adjourn to next Thursday.

Soph. We have sufficiently fatigued you for
this time, and we can never repay our obligations to you.

EVENING

EVENING VI.

Hortenſius, Sophronia, Euphraſia.

Hort. WELL met my fair friends,—I would not forego our weekly *Coterie,* for any route or aſſembly whatever.

Euph. You do us honour, and we will ſtrive to deſerve it.

Soph. The honour is all your own,—I diſclaim any ſhare of it.

Euph. I except it then as the reward of my labours; which I ſhall continue with the ſame, or increaſed aſſiduity.

Hortenſius I now deſire to hear your objections, to any part of what I have advanced in our paſt converſations?

Hort. Yes,—my objections to what has been ſaid by men of firſt-rate Genius, learning

ing, and judgment. You have contrived so as to transfer your attack from yourself to those, whom I dare not contradict.

Euph. If I have done it unfairly, I shall be ready to submit.

Hort. No, I dare not say so, nor do I mean to oppose you;—on the contrary, you have convinced me of some errors, and cured me of some prejudices. I confess I have not been conversant enough in this *Genus* of composition, as you have properly called it, to be a competent judge of the merit or defects of most of the works in it.—I come to you for further information, in pursuing the subject before us. You promised to proceed to your remarks on their effects upon the manners of their times respectively

Soph. Will you permit me first to ask a question?

Euph. As many as you please, Madam.

Soph. I have been desired to mention a certain book to you, and to ask if you have read it, and whether it would not be of service in your present enquiry?—It is called,

" Traité

" *Traité de l'Origine de Romans, par Monſ.*
" *Huet.*"

Euph. I have it my own library.

Soph. And what is your opinion of it?

Euph. I will give it you in the words of
Shakeſpeare.——

" His remarks are two grains of wheat in
" two buſhels of chaff, you ſhall ſearch for
" them a whole day, and when you have
" found them they are not worth your la-
" bour."

Soph. Shall I tell the gentleman who de-
ſired me to offer it to you, of this ſentence of
yours, or *Shakeſpeare's*?

Euph. Not ſo, I will put my anſwer into
the mouth of a great Critic, whoſe ſentence
will be as reſpectable, as it is deciſive.——

The ſupplement to the Tranſlator's preface
to *Jarvis's* Don *Quixote*, is ſaid to be written
by Biſhop *Warburton*, and would be no diſ-
credit to any writer. I ſhall read you the
paſſage I referr'd to.——

" Monſ. *Huet* Biſhop of *Avranches*, who
" wrote a formal treatiſe upon the Origin of
" Romances,

" Romances, has said little or nothing of
" them, in that *superficial* work.—Having
" brought down the account of Romances to
" the later Greeks, and enter'd upon those of
" the western writers, which have now the
" name of Romances almost appropriated to
" them, he puts the change upon his readers,
" and instead of giving us an account of these
" books of Chivalry, he contents himself
" with a long account of the poems of the
" Provencal writers, which are called like-
" wise Romances:—and so, under the equi-
" voque of a common term, drops his pro-
" per subject, and entertains us with another,
" that had no relation to it more than in the
" name."

Hort. She comes upon us with her extracts
again, and she uses them so as to make them
irresistable.

Soph. Will you give me a copy of this extract, to shew my friend.

Euph. With all my heart. I hoped to have
found many helps from this treatise, but was
disappointed. I expected an account of the
Milesian

Milesian Tales, which are often mentioned by those who treat on this subject, and I made a brief extract, of what fills many pages in Monf. *Huet*'s book.

He says that the Ionians were the most corrupt and diffolute of all the Asiatic Greeks,—that they fell under the dominion of *Cyrus*, when he conquered Asia Minor,—that the Perfians imbibed their manners, and became the most voluptuous people in the world. But, in them and a taste for elegant pleasures, the Milesians surpassed them all. They were the first that introduced Romance writing among the Perfians, which obtained the highest reputation in those times.—That the Milesian Fables are full of licentious stories and amorous adventures, which gave offence to those of the graver fort.—He thinks it probable that Romances were innocent till they fell into their hands, and that before that time they only recounted memorable and singular adventures. He says that their works are devoured by time, and yet, afterwards, advances several conjectures concerning them. If they

were

were fuch as he defcribes, they are beft buried
in oblivion.   It is the opinion of many learned men, that the works of *Lucian*, and likewife of *Apuleius*, are derived from thefe Mi-
lefian fables.

Monf. *Huet* runs over the names of many
fabulous and fome real Authors, but as they
are only names, they are of no great confequence.

Hort. Does he fay nothing of the compo-
fitions of later times?

Euph. Oh yes!—he extols the French Romances of his own times, as the moft perfect
of all works of this kind; and fays they deferve the fame compliment that *Horace* paid
to the Iliad of *Homer*,—that they teach Morality more effectually, than the precepts of
the moft able Philofophers.

Hort. Are not thefe the works we have juft
been criticifing?

Euph. The very fame.   I will only give
a fpecimen of his Style,—" Monf. *D'Urfé*
" was the firft who retrieved Romances from
" barbarity, and reduced them to rules in his
" incomparable

" incomparable *Aftrea*. The moft ingenious
" and polite work which has appeared in
" this kind, which eclipfed the glory which
" Greece, Italy, and Spain had acquired."

Hort. Well faid Bifhop!—you loved Romances as well as *Heliodorus.*

Euph. He goes on yet farther, and fpeaks
with admiration and aftonifhment of thofe of
Mademoifelle de Scudery.—" That the art of
" writing Romances (fays he) might be able
" to defend itfelf againft fcrupulous cenfures,
" not only by the commendations of the Pa-
" triarch *Photius,* but by the great examples
" of thofe who have applied themfelves to it,
" and might juftify itfelf by hers."

Soph. I am aftonifhed at what I have heard!

Euph. Oh pray liften to one more period,
which is in the true French ftyle of Hyperbole!
—" That that which had been improved by
" Philofophers, as *Athenagoras* and *Apuleius*;
" —by a Roman Prætor, as *Sifenna*;—by a
" Conful, as *Petronius*;—by an Emperor, as
" *Clodius Albinus*;—by a Prieft, as *Theodo-*
" *rus Prodromus*;—by Bifhops, as *Heliodo-*
" *rus*

" *rus*, and *Achilles Tatius*;—by a Pope, as
" *Pius Secundus*;—by a Saint, as *John Da-*
" *mafcenus*;—might have the honour to be
" attended to, by a wife and virtuous maid."

Soph. Hyperbole indeed!—I hope after
this, *Hortenfius* will read the Romances of
Mefdemoifelles Scudery.

Hort. I hope you will excufe me,—unlefs
you enjoin it as a penance for the trouble I
have given our ingenious friend.

Soph. I am in hopes, that this trouble may
turn to good account, and that our friend
may reap the fruits of her labours, in more
than one refpect,—and for this reafon, I excufe your penance.

Euph. We will fpeak of that hereafter.—
With your permiffion we will now proceed to
fome remarks on the effects of Romance upon the manners of their refpective times.

Hort. Pray do fo,—we are come fairly to
this point.

Euph. The extravagances and abfurdities
of Romances, have been pointed out by many writers, but few have attempted to fhew
the

the good effects they have produced.—Will you accept the Bifhop of *Avranches* as an advocate for them?

Hort. Not unlefs he fhews us in what refpect mankind are benefited by them.

Euph. Perhaps you expect too much, it is not eafy to demonftrate the effects of writings of fo mixed a nature. People muft read fomething, they cannot always be engaged by dry difquifitions, the mind requires fome amufement.—Story-telling is of ancient and reverend origin as I hope we have proved.— That thefe ftories fhould have a moral tendency will be generally allowed,—that they go frequently much higher, and when compofed by people of cultivated genius and virtuous principles, they fpeak to all the nobleft feelings of the human heart, and excite to fuch actions as they defcribe, of which I fhall give fome remarkable inftances. Give me leave to introduce to you a fet of men all of whom read, and fome of them wrote Romances :—men who, as all the world allows, had no fmall portion of Romance in their compofition, and were excited by a ftrong and enthufiaftic thirft of glory, to actions honourable to themfelves, and advantageous to their country. Such were the heroes of Queen *Elizabeth*'s court; and I might reckon the Queen herfelf as an Heroine, worthy to command fuch men.

Hort. You have well chofen this circle, for the illuftration of the fubject. The Prince who can felect, and employ fuch men, deferves the glory he derives from them ; and while he ufes their abilities, does himfelf the greateft honour.

Euph. Your obfervation is juft ; and there is no better Criterion of a Prince's abilities and principles, than the circle of men he draws round him.—Such was *Elizabeth*, and fuch were her fervants.—Sir *Philip Sydney*,— Sir *John Norris*,—the Earl of *Effex*,—Lord *Willoughby*,—Lord *Herbert* of *Cherbury*,— Sir *John Perrot*,—Sir *Francis Drake*,—Sir *Walter Raleigh*,—Admiral *Howard*,—Lord *Montjoy*,—Sir *Francis Vere*,—and many others.

Hort.

Hort. What a conftellation of Heroes!—
it make ones blood grow warm at the bare
mention of them.—When fhall we fee again
fuch men.

Euph. I will not anfwer your queftion, but
by telling you a Story.

The French army ufed to fing the fong of
Rolando or *Orlando*; to excite their courage
before a battle.—King *John* of France, (the
fame who died in England in 1364,) faid one
day, to thofe who had been finging this famous fong,—" It is a long time fince there
" has been any *Rolando*'s among the French."
—an old Captain made him the following
anfwer,—" Sire, we fhall fee again the *Ro-*
" *lando's*, when we have another *Charle-*
" *magne.*"

Hort. A word to the wife!—But did any of
thefe Heroes write Romances?

Euph. You have lately heard of Sir *Philip
Sydney*'s works.—Did you never read the life
of Lord *Herbert*, written by himfelf?

Hort. I have,—he is indeed a Hero worthy of Romance.

H 2

Euph.

Euph. He certainly was a copy of thefe models, and rather approaching to the cha-racter of Don *Quixote*; but his noble fpirit, and fine qualities, concealed or excufed his knight-errantry. Certainly thefe men were animated by great and generous principles, to expofe their lives continually to obtain what they thought infinitely more valuable,— an honourable name and memory. I have a curious book, of the lives and actions of Q. *Elizabeth*'s worthies, who were all men of this ftamp. I will give you an anecdote from thence, as a fpecimen of the fpirit of thofe times.

" The Lord *Montjoy* (above mentioned,)
" was of a bold and daring fpirit. When
" very young, he went abroad as a volunteer
" without the Queen's permiffion, for which
" he was feverely checked by her and forbid-
" den to do fo again;—notwithftanding this,
" he ftole away a fecond time, and went with
" Sir *John Norris* into *Brittany* and made a
" campaign there,—at his return the Queen
" reproved him fharply before the whole
　　　　　　　　　　　　　" court,

" court, in the following words.—Serve me
" so again, and I will lay you faft enough!—
" you will never leave, till you are knock'd
" on the head, like that rafh and inconfider-
" ate fellow *Sydney*.—It is time enough for
" you to go abroad when I fend you, till then
" ftay at home, read your books, and ftudy
" the art of war, againft you are called to
" the practice of it."

There is fomething in this afpiring fpirit
that affects one,—we cannot help admiring
and lamenting this enthufiafm of glory.

Oh fatal love of fame!—Oh glorious heat!——
Only deftructive to the brave and great!— ADDISON.

Hort. I admire with you, this avarice of
fame and glory,—it warms one's heart, with
a degree of their enthufiafm!—but furely
Madam, you do not affert that Romances infpired thefe men to perform all thefe great
actions?

Euph. They certainly had a great fhare in
them, you find yourfelf warmed at the bare
mention of them; and doubtlefs they were
excited by the great names they had heard
and read of.

The

The effects of Romance, and true History are not very different. When the imagination is raised, men do not stand to enquire whether the motive be true or false.—The love of glory has always a certain enthusiasm in it, which excites men to great and generous actions, and whatever stimulates this passion, must have the credit of the actions it performs. On the contrary, whenever this spirit, and this enthusiasm, become the objects of contempt and ridicule, mankind will set up for themselves an idol of a very different kind.—They will then devote themselves to mean or mercenary pursuits which debase and corrupt the mind.—The thirst of immoderate wealth or pleasure, will engross their attentions and desires; or else they will sink into a state of supine indolence, and become entirely negligent of what they owe to themselves, to their connexions, or to their country.— There must be a stimulus to excite men to action, and such as is the motive, such will the action be.

Hort. I confess that your reasoning is just, and I sigh over the comparison.—The ambition

tion

tion of our age, and country, is indeed of a very different kind.

Euph My favorite Romance-writer, *John Barclay*, deſcribes it as if he had lived in later times.—" The youth of our country, " ſays he, inſtead of deſiring to ſignalize " themſelves abroad, contract an avaritious " deſire of enriching themſelves at home, by " the ſpoils of their own country."

Hort. The painting is ſtrong, and the picture but too like.

Euph. Compare the times paſt with the preſent; and ſee on which ſide the balance will turn; in favour of public ſpirit, or private virtue.   Let us ſuppoſe the character of Don *Quixote* realized, with all its virtues and abſurdities.   I would aſk, whether ſuch a man is not more reſpectable, and more amiable, than a human being, wholly immerſed in low, groveling, effeminate, or mercenary purſuits, without one grain of private virtue, or public ſpirit; whoſe only thoughts, wiſhes, and deſires, are abſorbed in a worthleſs ſelf?

Hort. But is there no medium between theſe two extremes?

Euph. Doubtleſs there is,—but mankind are apt to run into extremes. We ridicule the enthuſiaſm of honour and glory, and run headlong into the gulph of folly and diſſipation,—we throw aſide forms and ceremonies, and ſink into careleſsneſs and negligence;—we deſpiſe decorum and preciſeneſs, and plunge into licentiouſneſs.

Hort. Who then ſhall draw the line?—who ſhall aſſign the bounds to faſhion, and bring it within the barriers of reaſon and morality. Oh honour, venerable and proſtituted name! —who ſhall aſcertain thee, and eſtabliſh thy dominion?—who ſhall put it out of the power of knaves and fools, to uſurp thy name, and wear thy trophies?—when ſhalt thou be reſtored to univerſal reverence?

Euph. That will be, when it is ſeen, as upon the reverſe of a Roman medal, with virtue for its inſeparable companion, with the old motto,—*Honos et Virtus.*

Soph. Bravo my friends!—It ſeems to me that you both have imbibed a good portion of the Enthuſiaſm you have deſcribed, and I have not heard you with inſenſibility.

Euph.

Euph. You do well to recall us to the subject of our conversation.   Romances have for many ages past been read and admired, lately it has been the fashion to decry and ridicule them; but to an unprejudiced person, this will prove nothing but the variations of times, manners, and opinions.—Writers of all denominations,—Princes and Priests,—Bishops and Heroes,—have their day, and then are out of date.—Sometimes indeed a work of intrinsic merit will revive, and renew its claim to immortality: but this happiness falls to the lot of few, in comparison of those who roll down the stream of time, and fall into the gulph of oblivion.

Upon the whole, I think, we may conclude, that Romances in general are neither the sublime compositions which their enthusiastic admirers have represented them; or so contemptible and pernicious as some prejudiced men have described them.—If upon a fair and impartial review of them, it appears, that they inculcated the greater principles of virtue and honour; though (in the

times

times of Gothic ignorance) they might be productive of many abfurdities, and fome real evils; yet they were by no means fo dangerous, as many writings of later times, of which I fhall have occafion to fpeak hereafter.

I have the courage to maintain that the moft eminent works of this clafs are entitled to our notice and refpect; and that even the moft heavy and prolix of them, are, at leaft, as innocent and inoffenfive, as any of the reft of the genuine offspring of dulnefs.

Hort. I entirely agree with you. I afk pardon for the injuries I have done them, and promife you that I never again will difturb their repofe.

Soph. I cannot forbear fmiling at his *Palinode*; it may be taken whatever way you pleafe to underftand it.

Euph. Then I fhall certainly take it the beft way.

Hort. I wifh you to take it in the way that does you moft honour: for I am fincerely obliged to you for the entertainment and information you have given me; and as foon

as

as your leisure will permit, I beg you to meet at my house and continue your progress.

Euph. I shall wait on you, as soon as I have collected materials, and I beg you to give me your assistance in future.

Soph. I sincerely wish it may be in my power to help you.—Adieu!

EVENING

EVENING VII.

Hortensius, Sophronia, Euphrasia.

Hort. WE have now, I presume, done with the Romances, and are expecting your investigation of Novels.

Euph. It is now that I begin to be sensible in how arduous an undertaking I have engaged, and to fear I shall leave it unfinished.

Hort. Have no fears, Madam; we shall not suffer you to leave off presently. We expect the completion of the plan you have given us.

Soph. If I judge rightly, the conclusion is yet a great way off.

Euph. This is one of the circumstances that frighten me. If I skim over the subject lightly it will be doing nothing; and if I am too minute I may grow dull and tedious, and tire my hearers.

Hort.

Hort. You must aim at the medium you recommended to us.

Euph. What Goddess, or what Muse must I invoke to guide me through these vast, unexplored regions of fancy?—regions inhabited by wisdom and folly,—by wit and stupidity,—by religion and profaneness,—by morality and licentiousness.—How shall I separate and distinguish the various and opposite qualities of these strange concomitants?—point out some as the objects of admiration and respect, and others of abhorrence and contempt?

Hort. The subject warms you already, and when that is the case, you will never be heard coldly.—Go on and prosper.

Euph. In this fairy land are many Castles of various Architecture.—Some are built in the air, and have no foundation at all,—others are composed of such heavy materials, that their own weight sinks them into the earth, where they lie buried under their own ruins, and leave not a trace behind,—a third sort are built upon a real and solid foundation, and

and remain impregnable againſt all the at-
tacks of Criticiſm, and perhaps even of time
itſelf.

Soph. So ſo!—we are indeed got into Fai-
ry-land; it is here that I expect to meet with
many of my acquaintance, and I ſhall challenge them whenever I do.

Euph. I hope that you will aſſiſt my labours.—I will drop the metaphor, and tell
you that I mean to take notice only of the
moſt eminent works of this kind:—to paſs
over others ſlightly and leave the worſt in the
depths of Oblivion.

The word *Novel* in all languages ſignifies
ſomething new. It was firſt uſed to diſtinguiſh
theſe works from Romance, though they have
lately been confounded together and are frequently miſtaken for each other.

Soph. But how will you draw the line of
diſtinction, ſo as to ſeparate them effectually,
and prevent future miſtakes?

Euph. I will attempt this diſtinction, and
I preſume if it is properly done it will be followed,—If not, you are but where you were
before,

before. The Romance is an heroic fable, which treats of fabulous persons and things. —The Novel is a picture of real life and manners, and of the times in which it is written. The Romance in lofty and elevated language, describes what never happened nor is likely to happen.—The Novel gives a familiar relation of such things, as pass every day before our eyes, such as may happen to our friend, or to ourselves; and the perfection of it, is to represent every scene, in so easy and natural a manner, and to make them appear so probable, as to deceive us into a persuasion (at least while we are reading) that all is real, until we are affected by the joys or distresses, of the persons in the story, as if they were our own.

Hort. You have well distinguished, and it is necessary to make this distinction.—I clearly perceive the difference between the Romance and Novel, and am surprized they should be confounded together.

Euph. I have sometimes thought it has been done insidiously, by those who endea-

vour

vour to render all writings of both kinds contemptible.

Soph. I have generally obferved that men of learning have fpoken of them with the greateft difdain, efpecially collegians.

Euph. Take care what you fay my friend, they are a fet of men who are not to be offended with impunity. Yet they deal in Romances, though of a different kind.—Some have taken up an opinion upon truft in others whofe judgment they prefer to their own.— Others having feen a few of the worft or dulleft among them, have judged of all the reft by them;—juft as fome men affect to defpife our fex, becaufe they have only converfed with the worft part of it.

Hort. You fex knows how to retort upon ours, and to punifh us for our offences againft you.—Proceed however.

Euph. The Italians were the firft that excelled in Novel-writing.—I cannot afcertain the date of any of their earlieft Novels. *Cynthio Giraldi*, and the Decameron of *Boccace*
are

are some of the first, and served as a model to many that were written afterwards.

Hort. One Original work of Genius, always produces a swarm of imitations.

Euph. *Cervantes* published his exemplary Novels in the year 1613.—They are twelve in number, and their titles are as follows:— *The little Gipsey—The liberal Lover—The Force of Blood—Ricconete and Cotadillo— The Spanish English Lady—The Glass Doctor —The jealous Estramaduran—The illustrious Chambermaid—The two Ladies—The Lady Cornelia—The deceitful Marriage—*I mention these by name, because (though they are well known) they have been introduced into other works and ascribed to other Authors. *Cervantes* boasts in his Preface, that he was the first that ever wrote Novels in the Spanish language, which is a proof that he intended them as a different species, from all his other works.

Hort. I make no doubt that the seed once sown, produced as plentiful a crop there, as it did in the rest of Europe.

VOL. I.   I   *Euph.*

Euph. No, I think not.—It went on fair
and softly in Spain, but in France it multiplied to infinity, as it has since done in England.—The first Novels in France were those
of *Scarron*, who probably took the hint from
Cervantes.—His Novels were soon buried
and forgotten, his best work is called *le Roman Comique*, which I imagine he intended as
a kind of Burlesque on the heroic Romance,
for otherwise, it is more properly a Novel,
than his other pieces.—It is very badly translated into English, by the Title of the *Co-
mical Romance*, whereas it ought to be the
Theatrical Romance, being the Adventures of
a company of strolling players;—under all
its disadvantages; it is still natural, lively,
and entertaining,

Soph. I have read an early Novel translated
from the French, which was much admired in
in its day, called *Zayde.*

Euph. I thank you for reminding me of it.
—It was written by M. *Segrais*, and the Treatise on the Origin of Romance by M. *Huet:*
was prefixed to it—in it the good Bishop pays

as

as many compliments to M. *Segrais*, as he does to M. *D'Urse* and Madamoif. *Scudery*.

Soph. But give us your opinion of *Zayde?*

Euph. It is fuperior to *Scarron*'s Novels, but I think, not equal to thofe of *Cervantes*; which have all ftrong marks of his Genius and fpirit.

Soph. Allow me to remind you of the *Princefs of Cleves*, the *Captives*, *Ines de Caftro*, and I fhall recollect others of the fame date.

Euph. You oblige me.—All the laft are within the limits of mediocrity, but the *Princefs of Cleves* is of worfe tendency, for it influences young minds in favour of a certain *fatality* in love matters, which encourages them to plead errors of the imagination, for faults of the heart, which if indulged will undermine both their virtue and peace.

Soph. You have not mentioned *le Sage ?*

Euph. *Le Sage* is indeed a writer of note, he is the Author of the *Devil upon Two Sticks*, (as the *Diable Boitu* is abfurdly tranflated,) of the *Bachelor of Salamanca*, and of *Gil Blas*, which is a Novel of firft rate merit.

Hort. There I agree with you.—*Voltaire* who never praises without good reason, speaks of it and its Author in these terms.—" *Son* " *Gil Blas est demeuré, parcequ'il y a du na-* " *turel.*"
—It is written in such a manner as to please all times and all people.—He speaks also of Novels written by Count *Antony Hamilton,* which were as lively as *Scarron*'s, without their Buffoonery.—Are you acquainted with his writings?

Euph. I have read his Memoirs of the Count *de Grammont,* which are written with the vivacity of a wit, and the ease of a fine gentleman; they are somewhat exceptionable on the score of morals, and yet as little as can be expected from the Memoirs of a li-centious court, that of *Charles* the Second, and the life of a man of pleasure like the Count *de Grammont.* I do not reckon this among the Novels, because it has truth for its foundation, though indeed highly embel-lished.—Of his Novels I know nothing, tho' I have made a strict enquiry after them, and I conjecture that they never were popular.

Soph.

Soph. I remember a book called *La Belle Assemblé*, that was very much read formerly, and I think it was well spoken of.

Euph. It was written some time after the books we have named, and it is a very unexceptionable and entertaining work of its kind. It carries marks of imitation of *Boccace*'s *Decameron*, and some of the stories are too far out of the limits of probability   Let us next confider some of the early Novels of our own country.

We had early tranflations of the beft Novels of all other Countries, but for a long time produced very few of our own.   One of the earlieft I know of is the *Cyprian Academy*, by *Robert Baron* in the reign of *Charles* the Firft.—Among our early Novel-writers we muft reckon Mrs. *Behn*.—There are ftrong marks of Genius in all this lady's works, but unhappily, there are some parts of them, very improper to be read by, or recommended to virtuous minds, and efpecially to youth.—She wrote in an age, and to a court of licentious manners, and perhaps we ought to afcribe to

I 3   thefe

these causes the loose turn of her stories.—Let us do justice to her merits, and cast the veil of compassion over her faults.—She died in the year 1689, and lies buried in the cloisters of Westminster Abbey.—The inscription will shew how high she stood in estimation at that time.

Hort. Are you not partial to the sex of this Genius?—when you excuse in her, what you would not to a man?

Euph. Perhaps I may, and you must excuse me if I am so, especially as this lady had many fine and amiable qualities, besides her genius for writing.

Soph. Pray let her rest in peace,—you were speaking of the inscription on her monument, I do not remember it.

Euph. It is as follows:

Mrs. APHRA BEHN, 1689.
Here lies a proof that wit can never be
Defence enough against mortality.

Let me add that Mrs. *Behn* will not be forgotten, so long as the Tragedy of *Oroonoko* is acted, it was from her story of that illustri-

ous

ous African, that Mr. *Southern* wrote that play, and the most affecting parts of it are taken almost literally from her.

Hort. Peace be to her *manes!*—I shall not disturb her, or her works.

Euph. I shall not recommend them to your perusal *Hortensius.*

The next female writer of this class is Mrs. *Manley,* whose works are still more exceptionable than Mrs. *Behn*'s, and as much inferior to them in point of merit.—She hoarded up all the public and private scandal within her reach, and poured it forth, in a work too well known in the last age, though almost forgotten in the present; a work that partakes of the style of the Romance, and the Novel. I forbear the name, and further observations on it, as Mrs. *Manley*'s works are sinking gradually into oblivion. I am sorry to say they were once in fashion, which obliges me to mention them, otherwise I had rather be spared the pain of disgracing an Author of my own sex.

Soph.

Soph. It muſt be confeſſed that theſe books of the laſt age, were of worſe tendency than any of thoſe of the preſent.

Euph. My dear friend, there were bad books at all times, for thoſe who ſought for them.—Let us paſs them over in ſilence.

Hort. No not yet.—Let me help your memory to one more Lady-Author of the ſame claſs.—Mrs. *Heywood.*—She has the ſame claim upon you as thoſe you have laſt mentioned.

Euph. I had intended to have mentioned Mrs. *Heywood* though in a different way, but I find you will not ſuffer any part of her character to eſcape you.

Hort. Why ſhould ſhe be ſpared any more than the others?

Euph. Becauſe ſhe repented of her faults, and employed the latter part of her life in expiating the offences of the former.—There is reaſon to believe that the examples of the two ladies we have ſpoken of, ſeduced Mrs. *Heywood* into the ſame track; ſhe certainly wrote ſome amorous novels in her youth, and alſo

also two books of the same kind as Mrs. *Manley*'s capital work, all of which I hope are forgotten.

Hort. I fear they will not be so fortunate, they will be known to posterity by the infamous immortality, conferred upon them by *Pope* in his Dunciad.

Euph. Mr. *Pope* was severe in his castigations, but let us be just to merit of every kind. Mrs. *Heywood* had the singular good fortune to recover a lost reputation, and the yet greater honour to atone for her errors.— She devoted the remainder of her life and labours to the service of virtue. Mrs. *Heywood* was one of the most voluminous female writers that ever England produced, none of her latter works are destitute of merit, though they do not rise to the highest pitch of excellence.—*Betsey Thoughtless* is reckoned her best Novel; but those works by which she is most likely to be known to posterity, are the *Female Spectator*, and the *Invisible Spy.*—this lady died so lately as the year 1758.

Soph.

Soph. I have heard it often said that Mr.
Pope was too severe in his treatment of this
lady, it was supposed that she had given some
private offence, which he resented publicly
as was too much his way.

Hort That is very likely, for he was not of
a forgiving disposition.—If I have been too
severe also, you ladies must forgive me in behalf of your sex.

Euph. Truth is sometimes severe.—Mrs.
Heywood's wit and ingenuity were never denied. I would be the last to vindicate her
faults, but the first to celebrate her return to
virtue, and her atonement for them.

Soph. May her first writings be forgotten,
and the last survive to do her honour!

Euph. Let us proceed to other writers.—
As I purpose in future to take notice only of
such Novels as are originals, or else of extraordinary merit, I must beg your allowance for
all trifling slips of memory, for errors in chro-
nology, and all other mistakes of equal consequence.—I must also have leave to mention
English and Foreign books indifferently, just

as

as they happen to rife to my memory, and obfervation.

Hort. It is but juft that you fhould have thefe, and every other allowance you can require, we have already laid a heavy tax upon you.

Euph. You fee I have many helps from my notes, and I hope to receive further affiftance from you both.——I will proceed with my progrefs. The life of *Cleveland*, natural fon of *Oliver Cromwell*, is one of the *old Novels*, if I may be allowed the expreffion, I do not certainly know the Author, nor yet the date of the firft edition.——When a Novel came out but feldom, it was eagerly received and generally read, this was at the time called a work of uncommon merit, but it will not bear a comparifon with thofe that have been written fince. There is originality and regularity in it. The incidents are too much of the marvellous kind, but fome of the fcenes are very pathetic, and there is bufinefs enough to keep the reader's attention conftantly awake,

and

and above all other merit, it has a moral tendency.

Hort. I have heard this book afcribed to *Daniel de Foe*, who as I think was alfo the Author of *Robinfon Crufoe*.

Euph. His title to the laft mentioned is not quite clear.—It is faid that he was trufted with a manufcript of *Alexander Selkirk*'s, who met with an adventure of the fame kind as *Crufoe*'s, and that he ftole his materials from thence, and then returned the manufcript to the Author—When *Selkirk*'s book was publifhed, it was taken but little notice of; it had more truth, but lefs Romance, and befide, the curiofity of the public was gratified, and they looked on *Crufoe* as the Original, and *Selkirk* as the copy only.

Hort. That was hard indeed, but I fear not unprecedented; you will give us your opinion of the book, exclufive of this circumftance.

Euph. *Robinfon Crufoe* was publifhed in the year 1720.—*Gaudentio di Lucca* in 1725. I fhall fpeak of thefe two books together,

because

becaufe there is a ftrong refemblance between
them, the fame marks of Originality appear in both.—They both give account of
unknown or rather of *Ideal* countries, but in
fo natural and probable a manner, that they
carry the reader with them wherever they
pleafe, in the midft of the moft extraordinary
occurrences. *Gaudentio di Lucca* is written
by the pen of a mafter, it is imputed to Bifhop *Berkely*, and is not unworthy of that
truly venerable man.—There is a greatnefs of
defign, and a depth of penetration into the
caufes of the health and profperity of a ftate,
and of the moral evils that firft weaken and
undermine, and finally caufe the ruin of it.—
The vaft confequence of the good or bad education of youth, on which depends the health,
vigour, and happinefs of a nation.—Thefe
circumftances gives this book a manifeft fupe-
riority to the other, in many other refpects they
are both equally entitled to our plaudit.—But
what gives a ftill higher value to thefe two
books, they are evidently written to promote
the caufe of religion and virtue, and may fafely
be

be put into the hands of youth.—Such books cannot be too ſtrongly recommended, as under the diſguiſe of fiction, warm the heart with the love of virtue, and by that means, excite the reader to the practice of it.

Hort. A warm plaudit you have given them,—I remember to have read *Robinſon Cruſoe* when very young, but I have forgot it, and ever ſince I have looked upon it as a book for children only; but I will read it again upon your recommendation, and judge of its merits.

Euph. That is the certain conſequence of putting theſe books too ſoon into the hands of children.—I will be bold to ſay a youth who reads them at a proper age, will never forget them.—Let me alſo beg you will read *Gaudentio di Lucca.*

Hort. I will certainly read them both at my beſt leiſure.

Soph. But let me beg you to get the old Edition of *Cruſoe*, for this is one of the books, which *Fanaticiſm* has laid her paw upon, and altered it to her own tenets, and ſhe has added ſome of her own reveries at the end of it,

called

called *Visions of the Angelical World*.—If *Hortensius* should once dip into that part of it, it would entirely discredit our recommendation.

Euph. You say true, I will get him the old Edition, which is the best.

Hort. Pray do you call these Books Romances or Novels?

Euph. They partake of the nature of both, but I consider them as of a different species from either, as works singular and Original. —I shall have occasion to place some later works under this class. But it is time for us to adjourn till next Thursday.

Hort. I shall not fail to meet you.

Soph. At my house.—No other engagement shall prevent it.

Hort. Agreed,—none could give me equal pleasure.

Euph. You are always my kind and indulgent friends, and your approbation is the crown of my labours.

EVENING

EVENING VIII.

Hortensius, Euphrasia, Sophronia.

Soph. MY good friends I rejoice to see you —We are now coming to a period within my memory and observation, and I shall ask *Euphrasia* a few questions.

Euph. As many as you please.—I expect your assistance.

Soph. Pray give us your opinion of the modern French Novels?

Euph. I will in a few words,—That the best are the most *excellent*, and the worst the most *execrable* of all others; and most of those I have read, fall under one or the other of these denominations.

Soph. You will give us your remarks upon the best of them.

Euph.

Euph. Are there any that you have particularly in view?

Soph. I was thinking of thofe of Monf. *Marivaux*—the *Payfan Parvenue*, and *Marianne*.

Euph. The works of *Marivaux* are of capital merit, they are pictures of real life and manners, and they have the advantages of highly polifhed language and fentiments; the *Payfan Parvenue* is fomewhat exceptionable, his French morality is not fuitable to an old Englifh palate, but his *Marianne* has no fuch abatements, "fhe needs no foil, but fhines by her own light."—It has indeed been tranflated into Englifh more than once, but never fo as to do juftice to the Original.

The firft was publifhed in 1742 it was a very poor literal tranflation, but yet it was read by every body with avidity; foon after another attempt was made by a ftill worfe hand, this is called *Indiana or the virtuous Orphan*, in this piece of patchwork, many of the fine reflexions, the moft valuable part of the work are omitted, the Story, left unfinifhed by the

VOL. I.   K   death

death of M. *Marivaux*, is finifhed by the
fame bungler, and in the moft abfurd manner.
It puts me in mind of what was faid to a certain tranflator of *Virgil.*

> Read the commandments friend,—tranflate no further,
> For it is written, thou fhalt do no murther.

Soph. Is the *Payfan Parvenue* tranflated
into Englifh?

Euph. It is, but not much better than *Marianne*, nor is it fo well known, it is frequent-
confounded with the *Payfanne Parvenue* of the
Chevalier *Mouhy*, which without half its merits is much more popular.—This laft work
has been twice tranflated, the firft bears the
title of *the fortunate Country Maid*, the fecond is called *the Virtuous Villager*, or *the
Virgin's Victory*, both are well known to the
readers of Circulating Libraries.

Hort. Did not M. *Crebillon* write fomething of this kind?

Euph. Les Egarément de Cœur et d'Efprit,
which was never popular in England, though
it was in France.—Some pious perfon, fearing
it might poifon the minds of youth (it is really exceptionable,) wrote a book of meditations.

tions with the same title, and *this* was the book that *Yorick*'s *fille de Chambre* was purchasing in the bookseller's shop.

Hort. All this is Greek to me——My intelligence came by reading Mr. *Gray*'s letters to his friends, in one of which he wishes to read eternally new Romances of *Marivaux* and *Crebillon*.

Euph. You find that Mr. *Gray* did not despise these books.

Hort. So it seems.——But he did not know how to call them.

Euph. That was because he never had read the true *Romances*, but confounded all fictions under that name; but I understand your meaning, and your raillery also.

Hort. I want to catch you tripping, but you always elude my traps.——Proceed, I will not interrupt you again impertinently.

Soph. Pray was not *Marianne* finished by Madame *Riccoboni?*

Euph. No—but I wish it had.——She wrote one of the books or divisions, to shew that she could write like M. *Marivaux*, and then gave it over.

Soph.

Soph. Don't you think Madame *Ricco-boni* a writer of great merit?

Euph. Capital.—Her Novels are first rates, and she wrote several pieces for the Stage with success.—I think *Jenny Salisbury* below the rest of her novels, because in it she attempted to paint English manners, without being sufficiently acquainted with them, and she has made strange work with English names and families.—Her letters of Madame *de Sancerre*—and *Valiere* are excellent,—and all her other works are in the first rank of Novels.

Soph. I have seen a collection of Novels published by Dr. *Croxall*, are they of any estimation?

Euph. They are an early selection of Novels, translated from the *Italian*, *Spanish* and *French* writers, of which we have made mention, none of them deserve farther particularizing.

Mrs. *St. Aubin*'s works are in the rank of mediocrity likewise.

M. *Prevot* was the Author of the *Marquis de Bretagne*, the *Chevalier de Grieux*, and
some

fome other pieces which belongs to the fame clafs.

Hort. You have not yet made mention of the moft eminent writers of our country, *Richardfon* and *Fielding.*

Euph. I hope you did not think it poffible for me to forget them. Mr. *Richardfon* publifhed his works, at a confiderable diftance of time from each other.—*Pamela* was the firft, it met with a very warm reception, as it well deferved to do.—I remember my mother and aunts being fhut up in the parlour reading *Pamela,* and I took it very hard that I was excluded.—I have fince feen it put into the hands of children, fo much are their underftandings riper than mine, or fo much are our methods of Education improved fince that time.

Soph. It is a general miftake in regard to the youth of our time, they are put too forward in all refpects. Let us return to *Pamela,* I can remember the time when this book was the fafhion, the perfon that had not read *Pamela,* was difqualified for converfation, of which it was the principal fubject for a long time.—You will give us your opinion of this, and the other works of Mr. *Richardson?*

Euph. To praise the works of Mr. *Richardson* is to hold a candle to the Sun, their merits are well understood in other countries besides our own; they have been translated into *French*, *Italian*, and *German*, and they are read in *English* frequently, by the people of the first rank in all the politest countries in Europe.

A Lady of quality in France, sent an Epigram to one of Mr. *Richardson*'s family soon after his death, which I will give you here.

> RICHARDSON tu nés plus!
> Le cœur humain en vous regret
> Son plus profound Observateur,
> Son plus eloquent interpret,
> Son plus parfait Legislateur.

I was desired to give a literal translation of it.

Hort. You will favour us with it I hope?

Euph. It is as follows:——

> RICHARDSON is now no more!
> Then may the human heart deplore
> Its most profound investigator,
> Its patron, friend, and regulator,
> And its most perfect Legislator.

Hort.

Hort. Very close indeed to the Original.

Soph. But your remarks on *Richardson's* works?

Euph. I will hazard a few remarks on them, which perhaps I may be allowed, because no person whatever has read them over with more pleasure and delight than myself.

It seems to me that *Pamela* is the *Chef d' Œuvre* of Mr. *Richardson.*—The Originality, the beautiful simplicity of the manners and language of the charming maid, are interest-ing past expression; and find a short way to the heart, which it engages by its best and noblest feelings.—There needs no other proof of a bad and corrupted heart, than its being insensible to the distresses, and incapable to the rewards of virtue.—I should want no other criterion of a *good* or *bad* heart, than the manner in which a young person was af-fected, by reading *Pamela.*

Euph. Your plaudit is a warm one.—But *Richardson* is a writer all your own; your sex are more obliged to him and *Addison*, than to all other men-authors.

K 4 *Euph.*

Euph. I deny that.—We have many other redoubtable champions as I shall bring proof enough,—and no man is degraded by defending us, for the female cause is the cause of virtue.

Hort. I mean not to degrade your champions or their cause.—But let us hear your critique on Mr. *Richardson*'s other works?

Euph. It was yourself who digressed from the subject. I have but little more to say of them; that all are of capital merit is indisputable; but it seems to me that *Pamela* has the most originality.—*Grandison* the greatest regularity and equality.—*Clariffa* the highest graces, and most defects.

Mr. *Richardson* was besides the first who wrote Novels in the Epistolary style, and he was truly an Original writer.

Hort. Have I your leave to make a few observations?

Euph. Certainly,—or to what purpose do we meet?

Hort. I allow the merit of this writer, and I respect his principles,—but I have some objections
jections

jections to the manner of his executing his designs.—1ft. His infupportable prolixity.—2dly. From his works have fprung up a fwarm of paltry Novels in the letter-writing way to the great exercife of our patience.—And 3dly, they have taught many young girls to wire-draw their language, and to fpin away long letters out of nothing.

Euph. You have given me materials for a longer difcuffion than the nature of our converfation will admit of, I will anfwer them as briefly as poffible.—To the firft objection,—Every man is to fpeak and write his own Eng-lifh, fome take a larger compafs than others, but if the language is good, and the end anf-wers the reader's time and attention, we have no right to complain.—If you have a mind to fee an Epitome of *Richardfon*'s works, there is fuch a publication, wherein the narrative is preferved; but you muft no longer expect the graces of *Richardfon*, nor his pathetic addref-fes to the heart, they are all evaporated and only the dry Story remains.—Perhaps this abridgement is the beft reply to your objec-

tion

tion.—To the fecond, No Author is anfwerable for faults of his imitators, and you have
before obferved that every Original writer is
followed by a fwarm of them, but you will
not furely for that reafon depreciate the Original writer.—To the third,—Let the young
girls bear the faults of the letters they write,
let them copy *Richardfon*, as often as they
pleafe, and it will be owing to the defects of
their underftandings, or judgments, if they
do not improve by him. We could not fay
as much of the reading Ladies of the laft age.

Soph. No truly, for their ftudies were the
French and Spanifh Romances, and the writ-
ings of Mrs. *Behn*, Mrs. *Manly*, and Mrs.
Heywood.

Hort. There is great weight in your obfervations, and yet I cannot but obferve that
you do not deny the force of my objections;
you only extenuate them,—but I will not
urge you to any farther reply at this time.—I
agree with you that no Author is anfwerable
for thofe effects, which his works are not intended to produce.

Soph.

Soph. Let me beg you to forbear any further digressions, and suffer *Euphrasia* to proceed in her progress without interruption.

Hort. I stand corrected Madam.—I beg you to proceed.

Euph. The next Author upon the lift, and whom *Hortensius* feared I should *forget*, is *Henry Fielding*, Esq. whose works are universally known and admired.—As I consider wit only as a secondary merit, I must beg leave to observe, that his writings are as much inferior to *Richardson*'s in morals and exemplary characters, as they are superior in wit and learning.—Young men of warm passions and not strict principles, are always desirous to shelter themselves under the sanction of mixed characters, wherein virtue is allowed to be predominant.—In this light the character of *Tom Jones* is capable of doing much mischief; and for this reason a translation of this book was prohibited in France.—On the contrary no harm can possibly arise from the imitation of a perfect character, though the attempt should fall short of the original.

Soph.

Soph. This is an indisputable truth,—there are many objectionable scenes in *Fielding*'s works, which I think *Hortensius* will not defend.

Hort. My objections were in character, and your's are so likewise; as you have defended *Richardson*, so I will defend *Fielding*.—I allow there is some foundation for your remarks, nevertheless in all *Fielding*'s works, virtue has always the superiority she ought to have, and challenges the honours that are justly due to her, the general tenor of them is in her favour, and it were happy for us, if our language had no greater cause of complaint in her behalf.

Euph. There we will agree with you.— Have you any further observations to make upon *Fielding*'s writings?

Hort. Since you refer this part of your task to me, I will offer a few more remarks.— *Fielding*'s *Amelia* is in much lower estimation than his *Joseph Andrews*, or *Tom Jones*; which have both received the stamp of public applause.—He likewise wrote several dramatic pieces

pieces of various merits, but these and his other works have no place in our present retrospect.—Lest you should think me too partial to the merits of this writer, I will give you the sentence of an historian upon him.

" The Genius of *Cervantes* (says Dr. *Smol-* " *let*) was transfused into the Novels of *Field-* " ing, who painted the characters, and ridi- " culed the follies of life, with equal strength, " humour and propriety."

Euph. We are willing to join with you in paying the tribute due to *Fielding*'s Genius, humour, and knowledge of mankind, but he certainly painted human nature as *it is*, ra- than as *it ought to be*.

Soph. These two last writers have detained your attention too long, I fear that you will cut us short for it on some future occasion. I grudge every digression that retards our progress.

Euph. The two last mentioned are of the first eminence, and had a claim to more than common notice; but though we sometimes take a compass, our work does not stand still

in

in the mean time, we will now proceed on our inquiry.——

Miſs *Sarah Fielding*'s works are not unworthy next to be mentioned after her brother's, if they do not equal them in wit and learning, they excell in ſome other material merits, that are more beneficial to their readers.—They well deſerve the protection of your ſex *Hortenſius*, and the plaudit of ours. The diſtinguiſhing marks of her beſt characters are ſimplicity of manners and benevolence of heart.

Hort. You muſt bring me acquainted with this lady's works, pray what are their titles?

Euph. The Hiſtory of David Simple—The Counteſs of Delwyn—Ophelia—Letters by the principal Characters in David Simple—The Lives of Cleopatra and Octavia—and laſtly, A tranſlation of Xenophon's Socrates, which is reckoned her capital work.

Soph. Pray did ſhe not alſo write a book, called, The Governeſs, or little Female Academy, for the uſe of Schools?

Euph:

Euph. I beg her pardon for omitting it. and I thank you for reminding me of it, for it does honour to the head and heart of the Author.—Miſs *Fielding* was one of thoſe truly eſtimable writers, whoſe fame ſmells ſweet, and will do ſo to late poſterity, one who never wrote " A Line that dying ſhe would " wiſh to blot."

Soph. What a pleaſure to pay the tribute due to ſuch a character!

Euph. How much happier, if one could ſtimulate others to imitate it!

Hort. You are ready enough to pay due reſpect to writers of your own ſex, but you are rather ſevere upon ſome of ours.

Euph. I hope not,—I wiſh to be impartial. But I will not begin an altercation with you at this time, leſt it ſhould interrupt our buſineſs, hereafter I will demand your objections, and endeavour to anſwer them all.

Hort. I deſire you will proceed in your own way.

Euph. It is time for us to adjourn.

Soph.

Soph. I am impatient to proceed in our progress, I forefee we are not near the conclufion, and though I wifh to get forward, I am in no hafte for the end.

Hort. Nor, I, believe me.—We meet at my houfe next Thurfday.

Euph. I begin to find this undertaking grow heavy upon me, I forefee many and great difficulties in my way, and am in doubt whether I fhall get to the end of my journey as I firft intended, or ftop fhort by the way.

Hort. Don't think of it, we fhall not fuffer you to ftop fhort.—Take a week's repofe, and you will return to your tafk with renewed ftrength and alacrity; and confider whether you cannot make more ufe of us, to lighten the burthen to you.

Euph. I thank you, and will confider of it, I will explain myfelf further at our next meeting.—I wifh you a good night!

Soph. I fhall think the time long till our next meeting. Adieu!

END OF THE FIRST VOLUME.

THE

PROGRESS of ROMANCE,

THROUGH
TIMES, COUNTRIES, AND MANNERS;

WITH

REMARKS

ON THE GOOD AND BAD EFFECTS OF
IT, ON THEM RESPECTIVELY;

IN A COURSE OF

EVENING CONVERSATIONS.

BY C. R. AUTHOR OF
THE ENGLISH BARON, THE TWO MENTORS, &c.

IN TWO VOLUMES.

VOL. II.

> IT hath bene through all ages ever seene,
> That with the praise of armes and chevalrie
> The prize of beautie still hath ioyned beene,
> And that for reasons speciall privitee,
> For either doth on other much relie :
> For he me seemes most fit the faire to serve,
> That can her best defend from villenie,
> And she most fit his service doth deserve,
> That fairest is, and from her faith will never swerve.
>
> SPENSER's Faery Queene. Book 4. Canto 5. Stanza 1.

PRINTED FOR THE AUTHOR,
BY W. KEYMER, COLCHESTER, AND SOLD BY HIM;
SOLD ALSO BY G. G. J. AND J. ROBINSON,
IN PATER-NOSTER ROW, LONDON,
MDCCLXXXV.

PROGRESS of ROMANCE.

EVENING IX.

Hortensius, Sophronia, Euphrasia.

Euph. A T our last meeting, I mentioned some difficulties I apprehended in my progress, as I should come nearer to the present times, and I must now confess, upon reflexion they increase.

Hort. Communicate them to your friends, and depend upon our best assistance, to obviate, or at least to abate them.

Soph. I sincerely wish it may be in my power to lighten the task to you.

Euph. We have hitherto travelled through these enchanted regions of fiction with tolerable ease and safety.—But as we advance further, new dangers awaits us every step we set.—We may tread upon serpents that may

A 2 rise

rife and fting us; or we may roufe a hornet's neft that may ftun us with its noife, or wound us with its deadly weapons.

Soph. Take us with you however, that we may know how to defend you.—Explain to us thofe dangers which perhaps are only ideal.

Euph. Alas, you will acknowledge the reality of them prefently!—The reputation of dead Authors is afcertained, and we may fpeak of their works with freedom and fafety; but it is not fo with living ones, we fhall fay too much or too little, either for them, or ourfelves.—As we advance, they multiply upon us, till they become a formidable army.

Soph. Let us meet them with the Olive in our hands, and promife to crown with laurels, thofe who beft deferve to wear them.

Euph. And who will think they do not deferve them?

Hort. Take courage *Euphrafia!* with truth and candour on your fide, you will make friends, who will be able and willing to defend you.

Euph.

Euph. With truth and candour on each side, that is yourfelf and *Sophronia*, I will endeavour to go forward warily and circumfpectly. —Firft then, I fhall only fpeak of the moft capital works of the kind, therefore I fhall have a demand for praife more than cenfure. —Secondly, I fhall fpeak *briefly* to their merits, and only enlarge upon thofe moft celebrated.—And Thirdly, I fhall fortify my own opinions, by the judgment of others of fuperior authority.

Hort. Since you have divided your heads f o methodically, give me leave to add another.—Fourthly, we will *(én dernier refort)* confult thofe infallible judges the *Reviewers*, as good Catholics do the Pope, and let them decide, where we defire to be excufed.

Euph. I thank you for that thought,—it will lighten my labour, and relieve my apprehenfions,—we will appeal occafionally to the moft candid and impartial of them, *viz.*—The *Monthly Reviewers.*

Soph. No more difqualifying, *Euphrafia.*— *Hortenfius*, no more fub-divifion,—let me beg

A 3 you

you to proceed, and not to abbreviate as you threaten us.

Hort. Come on then.—Let us *view* and *Review* your lift *Euphrasia.*

Euph. The *Female Quixote* was publifhed in the year 1752.—In this ingenious work the paffion for the French Romances of the laft Century, and the effect of them upon the manners is finely expofed and ridiculed.—The Author of it is fince well known as one of the diftinguifhed female writers this age has produced among us—Mrs. *Lennox.*

Soph. That circumftance is fo well known, that I fhall not be thought to detract from her merit, if I venture to remark, that the Satire of the *Female Quixote* feems in great meafure to have loft its aim, becaufe at the time it firft appeared, the tafte for thofe Romances was extinct, and the books exploded.

Euph. Your remark is juft,—this book came thirty or forty years too late.—But Mrs. *Lennox*'s character is eftablifhed upon works of a fuperior kind, which are above our retrofpect, though we can only fpeak here of her Novels.

—She

—She wrote two others, one called *Henrietta,* and the other *Sophia*—both of indisputable merit.

Hort. You are in the right Ladies.—Romances at this time were quite out of fashion, and the press groaned under the weight of Novels, which sprung up like Mushrooms every year.

Euph. They did but now begin to increase upon us, but ten years more multiplied them tenfold. Every work of merit produced a swarm of imitators, till they became a public evil, and the institution of Circulating libraries, conveyed them in the cheapest manner to every bodies hand.

Hort. I rejoice that you do not defend Circulating libraries,—if yon had, I would have fought against them with more success, than I have met with hitherto, when I have been your opponent.

Euph. I am entirely of your opinion, they are one source of the vices and follies of our present times; and we shall have occasion to say more of them when we come to draw in-

A 4   inferences

ferences from the effects of novel-reading upon the manners.

Hort. They have been well ridiculed in Mr. *Colman*'s farce called *Polly Honeycombe*.

Euph. In some respects, but the Satire would have been much stronger and the moral more commendable, if he had not exhibited the parents as objects of Ridicule; which spoils the effect, and puts it upon a footing with too many other Dramatic pieces upon the same plan.

Soph. I am delighted with your remark, and have often been offended with this dramatic error: it is so general that most of the plays seem calculated to teach our youth, that they are wiser than their parents, and that they may safely deceive and ridicule them.

Hort. You say true, there is hardly a play where one does not meet with these absolute children and undutiful parents, and the poets always take care to punish the latter, and reward the former

Euph. This likewise is one of the evils of our times; but we will not enlarge upon it here, as it is foreign to our present subject.

Soph.

Soph. I beg your pardon!—undutiful parents and arbitrary children are as frequently found in Novels as upon the Stage, and the remark is equally proper upon both kinds of writing.

Euph. I cannot deny it.—But I ſhall neither applaud, nor recommend any that have a tendency to weaken the reſpect due to parents; for upon that depends in a great meaſure, the education of youth, their introduction into life, and indeed all the ſocial and domeſtic virtues.

Hort. It was I that led you into this uſeful obſervation:—I do not repent it, nor will I reckon the time as loſt.

Euph. Let us however return into our proper track.—You will allow me to ſpeak of the works of the ſame Author together, though publiſhed at conſiderable intervals of time, to relieve my memory, and becauſe you may have them all in view at one time.

Hort. Certainly,—we can make no objection

Euph.

Euph. Whenever you recollect any books of this kind that are worthy of our notice, and that are not mentioned in my notes, you will oblige me by reminding me of them.

Hort. I will then put you in mind that Dr. *Smollet* was a novel writer.

Euph. Dr. *Smollet*'s Novels abound with wit, and humour, which some Critics think is carried beyond the limits of probability; all his characters are over charged, and he has exhibited some scenes that are not proper for all readers; but upon the whole, his works are of a moral tendency,—their titles are, *Roderick Random—Peregrine Pickle—Sir Lancelot Greaves—Ferdinand Count Fathom—Adventures of an Atom.*—Many years after these he gave the public another, in no respect inferior, and in some superior to them all, called *Humphrey Clinker.*

Hort. Honest *Humphrey* is an acquaintance of mine, and he is really a pleasant fellow.—But as you say many of the characters are *outrée.*

Euph.

Euph. Then you do condefcend to read Novels fometimes, efpecialiy when they are written by men?

Hort. Spare your raillery,—it was *Romances*
that I made war againft, and you have taught
me to make the proper diftinction.

Euph. I never meant to animadvert upon
fuch books as were capable of affording you
rational entertainment, it is only the Cynical
cenfurers of them that I reflect upon.—I will
mention another novel writer of your fex,
with a Dr. prefixed to his name likewife.—
Dr. *Shebbeare*'s Novels have fpirit, humour,
and morality, but their merits have great
abatements, on the fcore of party virulence,
and private fpleen.—His firft Novel was called the *Marriage-act*, which gave offence to
thofe who had a hand in compofing that *famous Act*, which makes an unfortunate *Æra*
in our manners. Whether he was profecuted,
or what other motive obliged him to alter the
Title I never could learn, but the fecond
Edition is called *Matrimony*—the other Novel
is *Lydia—or filial Piety.*

Hort.

Hort. It seems you dislike that *famous Act*, as much as *Shebbeare?*

Euph. I only read its motives, by its consequences, it is from this Æra, that we have seen the manners of the women of our country reflect disgrace upon it.—Trials of a certain kind, and Divorces in consequence, were very rare before that Period, and alas too common ever since!—I reason from facts, and they are stubborn things.

Hort. I am afraid there is too much truth in your remark,—our manners are indeed on the decline, and there needs no Act of Parliament to discourage marriage.

Euph. You are leading me away from my subject again.—I will look over my notes, and gather up the clue to our further progress. —I find the *Card* mentioned as a work of merit, it is an imitation of the different styles of our most eminent Novel-writers, it has wit, humour, and sentiment.—If I am rightly informed, it is the work of a Clergyman whose name was since much vilified; but as there is

no

no name prefixed to the book, I have no bufinefs to declare it.

Pompey the Little—a book much read and
admired, the Author likewife chofe to remain
unknown. It is a work of more than common merit.

Peter Wilkins—a work of Originality and
Morality, I fhall fpeak of it under a feparate
clafs.

Soph. I fee you are determined to keep up
to your laft regulation, and you abridge with
a vengeance.

Euph. I fhall do fo for the moft part, but
I will next mention a book, that will oblige
me to enlarge, and perhaps I may exercife
your patience.—I am going to fpeak of *Rof-
feau*'s new *Eloifa*.

Hort. Aye, truly that will afford an ample
fubject for Criticifm, let us hear what you
can fay upon it *Euphrafia:*

Euph. It is dangerous to criticife a work
that has been fo much, and fo juftly admired.
—It is a book that fpeaks to the heart, and
engages that in its behalf, and when reflexion
comes

comes aferwards, and reafon takes up the reins, we difcover that it is dangerous and improper for thofe for whofe ufe it is chiefly intended, for young perfons.

Hort. I expect a more particular examination of it, and a proof of your affertion.

Euph. It fhall then be in the words of another, as ufual *Hortenfius.*

Voltaire's *Prophecy* is at once the moft juft and fevere Satire upon it.—I have an extract of juft fo much of it as is requifite to my prefent purpofe, and in his opinion I give my own, expreffed to the utmoft advantage.

Hort. I muft bear with this extract, as I have with many others, but, I referve the liberty of replying to it.

Euph. That is but juft, liften to *Voltaire.* —" The Author of this book like thofe Em-
" piricks who make wounds on purpofe
" to fhew the virtues of their Balfams, poi-
" fons our fouls for the glory of curing them.
" And this poifon will act violently on the
" underftanding and on the heart, and the
" antidote will act on the underftanding only,
the

" and the poifon will triumph in the heart.—
" And he will boaft of having opened a gulph,
" and he will think he faves himfelf from
" blame by crying out.—Woe be to the young
" girls that fall into it!—and he will fay, I have
" warned you againft it in my preface, and
" young girls never read prefaces.—And he
" will fay by way of excufe for writing a
" book that infpires vice, that he lives in an
" age wherein it is impoffible to be virtuous.
" —And to juftify himfelf, he will flander
" the whole world, and threaten with his
" contempt all thofe who do not approve
" his book.—And every body fhall wonder,
" how with a foul fo pure and virtuous, he
" could compofe a book that is fo much the
" reverfe,—and many who believed in him
" fhall believe in him no more."

Hort. Poor *John James Rouffeau!* furely
thy brother *Voltaire* is too fevere upon thee,
not confidering his own flights and vagaries!

Euph. Will you undertake to defend him?

Hort. I will do like you, when your favourites are attacked, I will extenuate his faults.—

I

I will confider *Rouffeau* as a Philofopher and
a virtuous man; he is neither a libertine nor
an encourager of loofe morals, and upon your
own principles, he is not anfwerable for the
bad effects of his works.

Euph. A man cannot compofe an amorous
Novel without intending it.

Hort. Perhaps his defign may be mifun-
derftood and mifconftrued.

Rouffeau faw that the women on the Con-
tinent, while maidens, paid due refpect to
their honour and character, but as foon as they
were married they entertained all the world,
and encouraged gallants; of the two evils
he thought a fingle perfon's indulging a criminal paffion, of lefs pernicious confequence
to fociety, than a married woman who com-
mits adultery :—upon this principle he wrote
this book.—He puts the character of a woman who encourages lovers after marriage, in
oppofition to one who having committed the
greateft fault before marriage, repents, and
recovers her principles.—He inforces the
fanctity of the marriage vow, he fets the
breach

breach of it in a light to shock every confi-
derate mind, he shews that where it is broken,
nothing but hatred and disgust succeeds; the
confidence a man should place in his wife, the
tenderness he should feel for his offspring,
is destroyed, and nothing remains but infamy
and misery.

If *Rousseau* intended by this work to give
a check to this shameful intercourse of the
sexes, so frequently practiced on the Conti-
nent, under the specious name of gallantry,
he is to be commended; and if it produced
effects he did not foresee, he ought to be ex-
cused.

Euph. I am sure *Rousseau* is much obliged to
your sensible and polite apology for his *Eloise*. But after all the objections remain. It is
a dangerous book to put into the hands of
youth, it awakens and nourishes those passions,
which it is the exercise of Reason, and of Religion also, to regulate, and to keep within
their true limits. On this account I have often wished that the two first Volumes of *Eloise*,
could be abridged and altered, so as to render

them

them confiftent with the unexceptionable morals of the two laft.—I thought it might be
poffible to give a different turn to the ftory, and
to make the two Lovers, ftop fhort of the *act*,
that made it criminal in either party to marry
another, for were they not *actually wedded* in
the fight of heaven? and could *Eloife* with
any pretenfions to virtue, or to delicacy, give
herfelf to another man?

If this infuperable objection was removed;
then might the Lovers renew their friendfhip
with honour and dignity on both fides, then
might the hufband in full confidence in his
wife's principles, invite her friend, and even
leave them together without appearing fo
juftly-ridiculous in his conduct as he now does
to impartial judges.

Hort. I like your plan, and advife you to
make this alteration yourfelf.

Euph. You muft excufe me Sir,—I have
not yet the prefumption to attempt it, or to
think myfelf able to do juftice to *Rouffeau*
in fuch an alteration.—It muft remain as it
is, it has done all the mifchief in its power to
the

the youth of this generation; and the worft part of it is, that thofe who write only for depraved and corrupted minds, dare appeal to *Rouffeau* as a precedent.

Hort. In that light I fee the bad effects of it manifeftly, and I believe that *Rouffeau* himfelf would be concerned for them;—but what will you fay of his *Emilius?*

Euph. Nearly the fame as of the other,—it may do fome good, but I am afraid much more harm.   The difcuffion of its merits and defects would lead me too far from the prefent fubject, efpecially as it does not properly belong to this clafs of writing.—*Rouffeau* is a whimfical and chimerical writer, with great beauties and great blemifhes, and I am convinced he did not really intend to hurt the principles or morals of mankind.

Hort. You do him barely juftice; but can you fay fo much of *Voltaire* who fo cruelly fcourges him?

Euph. No truly.—He never miffes an opportunity of fhewing his wit, and his malignity, likewife, againft Revelation; and in doing injury to Religion, he injures the rights and the happiness of society.

Soph. It is pleasant to see these Freethinkers and free speakers, throwing dirt at each other:—to see the Author of *Candide* taking exceptions at the character of *Wolmar*.

Hort. Your remark is good, and reminds me of a vulgar proverb, "When knaves " quarrel, honest men recover their own."— Thus a Christian may know what confidence to place in the enemies of his religion.—But pray give us your opinion of *Candide?*

Euph. Not I indeed, let the *men* do it.— Pray *Hortensius* look for what the Reviewers say of it.

Hort. Here I have it,—*Monthly Review,* 1761—" *Candide, or, All for the best.*—An " absurd improbable tale, written with an ap- " parent view to depreciate not only human " nature, but the wisdom and goodness of " the Supreme Being; and ridicule his pro- " vidence under that generally received and " worthily adopted principle—All for the " best."—Gramercy Messrs. the Reviewers.

I

I subscribe to your sentence with all my heart.

Euph. *Hortensius* you have led me to speak of *Voltaire*'s works, which I would rather have avoided: his wit is indisputable, but wit is only a secondary merit; and when it is abused and made an instrument to do mischief, it becomes detestable.

Hort. It was impossible to avoid speaking of him as a writer of eminence in your walk, —and will you say nothing more of his Novels?

Euph. Nothing.—I do not wish to recommend them, they will always be found by those, who think it worth their while to seek them.

Soph. Let us leave them to their admirers. —It is time for you to pursue your journey, and to mention other writers.

Euph. Or rather, it is time to separate for this evening, the next time we meet, we must make quicker dispatch, or this progress of ours, will be too long before it comes to an end.

Hort. I believe you will be tired the first of the party.

Euph. If I do not tire my hearers I shall be satisfied.—A good night to you.

EVENING

EVENING X.

Hortenfius, Sophronia, Euphrafia.

Euph. YOU are truly welcome my friends.—I receive you in my library, becaufe we fhall want to have recourfe to our books.

Hort. Make me your Librarian, or employ me in fome way as your affiftant.

Euph. I make ufe of your permiffion, pray take down the *Monthly Review* for the year 1761—and look for *Sidney Biddulph.*

Soph. This looks like doing bufinefs;— but pray do not transfer your tafk to the Reviewers.

Euph. Never fear, there will ftill remain employment enough for me.

Hort. I have it here —" In the work be- " fore us, the Author feems to have defigned

" ed to draw tears from the reader by diftref-
" fing innocence and virtue as much as pof-
" fible.—Now though we are not ignorant
" that this may be a true picture of human
" life in fome inftances; yet we are of opi-
" nion that fuch reprefentations are by no
" means calculated to encourage or promote
" virtue."

Euph. Stop there if you pleafe, I do not
want the whole Article. I have in my notes
an extract from the *Critical Review*, which
will be a proper contraft to the other.

" The defign of this work is to prove that
" neither prudence, forefight, nor even the
" beft difpofition the human heart is capable
" of, are of themfelves fufficient to defend
" us from the inevitable evils to which hu-
" man nature is liable.—Whether this infer-
" ence is favourable to the encouragement of
" virtue, we could not ftop to enquire: we
" were fo interefted in the diftrefs of *Sidney*
" *Biddulph*, and fo abforbed in the events of
" her life, that in fhort, every arrow of Cri-
" ticifm was unpointed.—Inftead of think-

ing

" ing thefe evils were allotted to her, we per-
" ceive that they arofe from a want of
" knowledge of the world, from too eafy cre-
" dulity, and from unfufpecting innocence.
" —We can only wifh that few of our read-
" ers may want her example to infpire and
" direct them."—You have heard the evidence on both fides and now I afk *your* opini-
nion *Sophronia?*

Soph. I had rather you had given your
own, but as you defire it I will.—This book
is a great favorite of mine, the Story is admi-
rably told, and the language is fo eafy and natural, that every thing feems real in it, and
we forrow as for a well known and beloved
friend; in my opinion it well deferves the en-
comium the Critical Reviewers have given it.

Hort. It is worthy of obfervation, that laying afide the dictatorial ftyle of Cenfors, they
fpeak of it, as if it was a true hiftory.—
" Inftead of thinking thefe evils were *al-*
" *lotted* to her, we perceive that they *arofe*
" from want of knowledge of the world, &c."
—I cannot help fmiling at it.

Euph.

Euph. Your obfervation is *deep* as well as *pleafant*, perhaps there is not a better Criterion of the merit of a book, than our lofing fight of the Author.

Hort. You have really converted my remark into folid value, and I readily agree to your criterion.

Soph And fo do I.—But I am miftaken if *Euphrafia* had not a further meaning in applying to me for my opinion of this book.— I am fond of melancholy ftories, and fhe prefers thofe that end happily, fhe meant to oblige me to declare my fentiments, and afterwards give her own; and then afk you to decide upon them.

Euph. I find you know my meaning by my gaping.—I do really think that books of a gloomy tendency do much harm in this country, and efpecially to young minds;— they fhould be fhewn the truth through the medium of chearfulnefs, and led to expect encouragement in the practice of the focial duties, and rewards for virtuous actions.

If

—If they fhould be unfortunate, they will fee the reverfe of the medal foon enough.

Hort. But will not the expectations of nothing but peace and happinefs, difqualify them to fuftain the reverfe ?

Euph. I fhould think not.—The mind that is always ruminating upon the evils of life, will be apt to caft every object into fhade.

Soph. Authors of the firft eminence have written upon both principles, and if your doctrine was to be followed, we fhould have no Tragedies, and no pathetic ftories.—What fays *Hortenfius?*

Hort. There is much to be faid on both fides; I do not prefume to decide upon the fubject.—But for myfelf, I fubfcribe to *Euphrafia's* opinion, that virtue ftands in need of every encouragement, confidering the many trials we muft encounter in her conftant warfare.—That youth fhould be led to expect the rewards of virtue in the prefent life, without lofing fight of a better expectation hereafter : and this will be a powerful antidote againft the unavoidable evils of life.—

Virtue

Virtue fhould always be reprefented in the moft beautiful and amiable light, capable of attracting the hearts of her votaries, and of rewarding every facrifice they can make to her :—but in truth there are too many moralifts (and I might add divines,) who reprefent her in fo auftere and difgufting a manner, as to difcourage and frighten her pupils away from her prefence.

Soph. Give me leave to mention one more book of this kind, which has been univerfally read and applauded.—*Raffelas Prince of Abyffinia.*

Euph. I have not forgotten *Raffelas*, I affure you, but I intended to place him in a different clafs.—However as he is upon the table, let us hear what the Reviewers fay of him?

Hort. " This book (fay they) was general-
" ly read and approved, the invention and
" language are worthy of the Author, (Dr.
" *Johnfon*) neverthelefs it leaves the mind
" gloomy and diffatisfied.—The inferences
" that happinefs is always in profpect and
never

" never attainable, is so discouraging a truth,
" *if it be one*, that it ought rather to be con-
" cealed, or at least softened to us.—Instead
" of directing our pursuits, it tends to keep
" us in a state of total inaction, whereas we
" want to be excited to activity, and made to
" expect our happiness in doing our duty,
" rather than to encourage us to remain in a
" state of inactivity and indolence."

Soph. It is clearly against me, and I must give up the point, rather than detain you any longer on the subject.

Euph. Not so my friend,—every one has a right to choose his books, and to judge for himself in these matters; there have been many eminent Poets and Painters who have chosen melancholy subjects, and they meet with as many admirers, as the more chearful ones, perhaps both may be useful to different dispositions, some minds want to be encouraged and comforted; others to be humbled and softened, by a retrospect of the evils to which human nature is liable.

Hort.

Hort. A very fair and generous compromise. You may refume the conteft at fome future time, when it does not interfere with the fubject before you.

Euph. I take up my clue again.—The year following two books of the fame kind were publifhed, both of them were in fome degree copies of *Raffelas*, but neither of them equal to it, though both had their refpective merit and admirers.—*Almoran* and *Hamet* by Dr. *Hawkefworth*, and *Soliman* and *Almena* by Dr. *Langhorne*, they both end happily *Sophronia*, and yet I prefer *Raffelas* to either of them.

Soph. I receive it as proof of your impartiality.

Hort. Do you know that you have pafs'd by a book more read and talked of than moft of thofe we have reviewed.

Euph. Likely enough, we have not been quite regular in our progrefs, but pray who is the great perfonage omitted?

Hort. No lefs a man than *Triftram Shandy*, Gent.

Euph.

Euph. I muſt beg of *you* to decide upon its merits, for it is not a woman's book.

Hort. Indeed I will not allow of your excuſe.—You have ſpoken freely enough of many other writers, and if you are a competent judge of them, why not of *Sterne?*

Euph. You urge me cloſely,—in verity I have never read this book half through, and yet I have read enough to be aſhamed of. Faſhion which countenances every folly, induced me to begin it;—but what what can I ſay of it with ſafety?—That it is a Farrago of wit and humour, ſenſe and nonſenſe, incoherency and extravagance.—The Author had the good fortune to make himſelf and his writings the *ton of the day*, and not to go out of faſhion during his life.—What value poſterity will ſet upon them I preſume not to give my opinion of, it is time that muſt decide upon them, and it will certainly do them juſtice.

Hort. You are very reſerved in your judgment of *Triſtram*, but what have you to ſay againſt his *Sentimental Journey?*

Euph.

Euph. It is indisputably a work of merit.—
Where *Sterne* attempts the Pathos, he is irresistable; the Reviewers have well observed,
that though he affected humour and foolery,
yet he was greatest in the pathetic style.—
His *Maria* and *le Fevre*, and his *Monk*, are
charming pictures, and will survive, when all
his other writings are forgot.

Hort. Then I am friends with you again,
which I could not be, if you had passed over
his merits, as slightly as his absurdities.

Euph. *Sterne*, like all other Original writers has been followed by a swarm of imitators,
not one of which deserve mention among
works of eminence in this class of writing.

Hort. Aye, let them sleep in peace. It
would ill become you who have passed over
the Novels of *Voltaire*, to mention this crop
of mushrooms.

Euph. I am deaf of that ear *Hortensius*,
and you know the cause of it—Let us take
leave of *Tristram*, and return to my list.—The
name I read is—*Longsword Earl of Salisbury*
an Historical Romance.

Hort.

Hort. How is that, a Romance in the 18th Century?

Euph. Yes, a Romance in reality and not a Novel.—A ſtory like thoſe of the middle ages, compoſed of Chivalry, Love, and Religion.—Pray turn to the *Review*, where I think you will find a high character of it.

Hort. A high character indeed!—" In this " agreeable Romance, the truth of Hiſtory " is artfully interwoven with entertaining fic- " tions, and intereſting epiſodes.—It ſeems " to be formed on an intimate acquaintance " with the Romances of the 15th and 16th " Centuries, which however extravagant and " beyond nature, were always favourable to " the cauſe of virtue, and are ſo far pre- " ferable to the more natural productions of " later times.—There is a certain pomp of " diction, a richneſs, and at the ſame time a " ſimplicity of expreſſion, which ſeldom fails " to captivate the reader, and particularly " impreſſes young minds, naturally warmed " and attracted by the ſplendor of the he- " roic virtues, and moved by the fineſt af-
" fections

" fections of the human heart.—In short,
" however the good old Romances may be
" now laughed out of doors, certain it is,
" that no species of writing could amuse with
" less injury to the morals, and virtuous man-
" ners of the Reader."—Why the Reviewers
speak your own sentiments!—I never suspect-
ed that you were in league with them

Euph. When they speak the language of
truth, candor and impartiality, I am always
ready to adopt their sentiments.—This work
is distinguished in my list, among Novels uncommon and Original.

Soph. It seems to me that you have passed
over several works of first rate merit.—*Longsword* was published in 1766.

Euph. I thank you heartily for reminding
me, I have skipped over a whole page in my
list, and my notes upon it.

I find that Mrs. *Sheridan* was the Author of
Sidney Bidulph, and also a very pretty Eastern Tale called *Nourjahad*.

Mrs. *Brooke*'s works hold a very high
rank in the Novel Species.—She first trans-

lated Lady *Catesby's Letters*, and afterwards
gave us two Novels of her own very much
superior to it, *Lady Julia Mandeville*, and
Emily Montague.—She also translated the *Marquis dé St. Forlaix*. Her stories are interesting and pathetic, her language highly polished and elegant.

Soph. Indeed Mrs. *Brooke*'s Novels deserve
all that you can say of them.—Pray did not
Millenium Hall come out about this time?

Euph. It was in the year 1762.—Mrs.
Brooke's works were published at different
times, *Emily Montague*, in 1763.

Soph. Have you nothing more to say of
Millenium Hall than the date of it?

Euph. It is a very good little book, and
you ought to have made its Eulogium.

Soph. I had rather hear my favourite's
praises from another mouth than my own.

Euph. Then I will pay it the homage it
justly claims. It is calculated to inspire the
heart with true benevolence and the love of
virtue, it is a very entertaining as well as moral

ral work, and very proper to be put into the hands of young perſons.

Soph. I am glad you think it worthy of a place in your claſs of eminence, for I am fond of it to a degree.

Hort. Now Ladies you have the whole buſineſs to yourſelves, I have not read any of the laſt mentioned books but *Emily Montague*, which indeed deſerves your plaudit.

Euph. The letters of *Theodoſius* and *Conſtantia* are both moral and entertaining, and they are alſo inſtructive, and deſerve a place in every good young woman's cloſet,— they came out 1763.

Hort. I would fain be of ſome uſe, pray are *Marmontel's* works, worthy of a place upon your ſhelf?

Euph. I could be offended at that queſtion, and more at the manner of it, and yet I will not ſpare what deſerves correction, *Marmontel* is as you well know, a charming writer, but his *Moral Tales*, have ſome things in them that are offenſive to *good Morals.*—His *Belliſarius* is worthy of a place in every Monarch's

C 2 Library

Library.—And his *Incas* to be enfhrined in. every benevolent heart.

Hort. I really beg your pardon.—I ought not to have *feemed* to doubt that you would do juftice to *Marmontel?*—I did not *really* doubt it.

Euph. I accept your Palinode.—I do not wifh to make a *Parade* of fentiment, like fome writers, who have brought even the word it-felf into difgrace. You know that upon *prin-ciple* I refufed to admit works of prophane-nefs and immorality into my Catalogue of eminent Novels, though admired for their wit, or for the name of the Authors; I fhould be concerned to have occafion to repeat any more what I have faid on this fubject.

Hort. I am forry to have given you occa-fion for what you have now faid.—Forget it, and proceed with your progrefs.

Euph. The next work of merit and mo-rality that I fhall fpeak of, is the *Marquis de Rofelle*, by Madame *Elie de Beaumont*. I have a partiality for this book, I never read one of the kind that afforded me greater pleafure;

pleasure; in it the noblest lessons of virtue and good conduct are conveyed to the reader's mind, through the vehicle of entertainment; it may be recommended to young persons, to guard them against the deceptions of the world, and to enable them to distinguish between real and intrinsic merit, and the tinsel accomplishments of the circle of dissipation. —This translation was published in 1764.

Soph. It is indeed, a charming book, and I think there are more writings of Madame *de Beaumont* worth your notice.

Euph. You will please to *observe*, that there are two Ladies of that name, with only a small distinction between them—Madame *Elie de Beaumont* is the Author of the *Marquis de Roselle.*—Madame *le Prince de Beaumont* has written many books for the use of Schools *Le Magazin des Enfans* and others for youth in a series.—She has also written *Novels for grown Gentlemen and Ladies*, but none of first rate Merit.

Soph. Is there not a book of her's called the new *Clarissa?*

C 3 *Euph.*

Euph. There is, but it is out of the bounds of nature and probability; there is also a book of the same title, which was published in Ireland, which I think superior to the French one, but neither of them are capital. —Madame *le Prince de Beaumont*'s writings are strongly tinctured with bigotry and enthusiasm, but she always means to support the cause of virtue.—If I am not misinformed she presides over a seminary of Education, or in plain English, she keeps a school.

Soph. An employment of great utility and importance, and when faithfully discharged, claims our respect, and an honourable mention.

Euph. Certainly, and deserves more respect than is generally paid to it—The year 1766 was very prolific in the Novel way, and indeed, they seem to have over-run the press, till they became a *drug* in the *terms* of *trade*.— The Reviewers complain bitterly of the fatigue of reading them, it became necessary to have an Annual Supply for the Circulating Library, in consequence the manufacturers of

Novels

Novels were conſtantly at work for them, and were very poorly paid for their labours.—Among the traſh the preſs groaned under, ſome works of merit appeared which diſcredited the trifling ones, and helped to drive them off the Stage.

Sir George Elliſon, a picture of a truly benevolent man.

Sir Charles Beaufort, ſtrong painting of ſhocking characters, which are made triumphant over Innocence and Virtue

John Buncle, *Eſq.*—a whimſical and *outré* ſtory, intermixed with ſprinklings of wit and Learning, and a Genius truly original.

The Vicar of Wakefield, by Dr. *Goldſmith*, a work of great merit and great faults, but muſt ever afford both pleaſure and benefit to a good heart.

Soph. Theſe laſt mentioned are abridged in good earneſt.

Euph. I find it neceſſary, and ſhall continue to do ſo except in particular caſes.

The fair American—or *Emmera*, a work of merit and morality, 1767.

Letters

Letters of Madame de Sancerre, by Madame *Riccobini*, which is saying enough.

History of Ernestina,—a very pretty story by the same Lady.

Lucy Watson, a melancholy tale well told as a warning to youth.

Hort. You drive away at a great rate, and I wish not to check your course, I shall come up to you, when you come to the inferences.

Euph. The *Life and Adventures of Common Sense*, is a work of Genius, wit, humour and morality, and will afford an agreeable entertainment to every reader of taste and judgment.

Arthur O'Bradley has more humour, than wit or sentiment, but is above the common Novels of this date—1769.

The Persian Tales of Inatulla are worth reading, but I shall class them with other Tales and Fables of the same kind.

Soph. You will do right to make them a separate class.

Euph. At this period when a constant supply of Novels was expected by the Readers of the

the Circulating Library, some persons whose excellent principles led them to see and lament the decline of virtuous manners, and the passion for desultory reading; endeavoured to stem the torrent by making entertaining stories their *vehicle* to convey to the young and flexible heart, wholsome truths, that it refused to receive under the form of moral precepts and instructions, thus they tempered the *utilé* with the *dulcé*, and under the disguise of Novels, gave examples of virtue rewarded, and vice punished; and if the young mind unawares to itself, was warmed with the love of virtue, or shocked at the punishment of the wicked; this was all the reward they wished or expected from their Labours.

Of this kind are the following works:

Callistus, or *the Man of Fashion,* by Mr. *Mulso.*

The Exemplary Mother, by Mrs. *Cooper.*

The Placid Man, by Mr. *Jenner.*

The Fool of Quality, by Mr. *Brooke.*

This last I must enlarge upon.—Mr. *Brooke* was a man of Genius, taste and sensibility, but

but unhappily thefe fine talents were over-
fhadowed by a veil of Enthufiafm, that cafts
a fhade upon every object.

I will not truft myfelf to give a character
to works of fo mixed a kind. Let us fee
what the Reviewers fay of it, *Hortenfius*, be
fo kind to turn to the Index for *The Fool of
Quality*.

Hort. I obey you Madam.—" While with
" pleafure we contemplate the amiable and
" worthy characters drawn by this able writer,
" it is with real concern that we fee them
" debafed by the afcetic reveries of Madame
" *Guyon*, *William Law*, and the reft of the
" rapturous tribe.—What can we fay more
" of a performance, which is at once en-
" riched by Genius, enlivened by fancy,
" bewildered with enthufiafm, and overrun
" with the visionary jargon of fanaticifm?

" We fhall only add our hearty wifh that
" the ingenious writer, would give us an
" abridgement of this work, cleared from the
" fanctimonious rubbifh by which its beauties
" are fo much obfcured ;—and then, we are
                              " perfuaded

" perfuaded, it would be perufed with plea-
" fure by readers of *every* rank and age; but
" while it remains in its prefent motley ftate,
" we apprehend it will be a favourite with
" only *Behmenites*, *Hernhutters*, *Methodifts*,
" *Hutchinfonians*,—and fome *Roman Ca-*
" *tholics*.

Euph. Very juft.—the fame character will
ferve for *Juliet Grenville*, Mr. *Brooke*'s other
Novel in which fanaticifm is predominant.
I fhall offer a conjecture of my own, that
Mr. *Brooke* would never have condefcended to
write Novels, but to make them his vehicles
to convey his *tenets* to the minds of fuch
readers, as were not likely to receive them
in any other form.

Soph. What a pity, that fuch genius and
fuch tafte fhould be ufed only to promote a
blind and illiberal zeal to make profelytes!
and to limit the mercies of God to one particular fect of Chriftians.

Hort. It is the characteriftic of the fects
enumerated in the *Review*.—The growth of
fanaticifm is an alarming confideration; it

                                    is

is creeping into every sect among us, nay even into the established national Church.

Euph. Between Deism on one hand, and fanaticism on the other, people of rational piety, and moderation, are in no very good situation, for they are anathemiz'd by the zealots of both parties.—Let us leave them to him who knows best how to separate the *grain* from the *chaff*, and return to our subject.

Letters from an English Lady at Paris, in which are contained *the Memoirs of Mrs. Williams.*—1769.

This is a work of real merit, I have here an extract from the *Review.*— 'The whole of
" this work forms a most interesting, exem-
" plary tale, abounding with affecting in-
" cidents, sensible observations, and moral
" reflections:—and some of the letters are
" enlivened with a vein of pleasantry, which
" will afford an agreeable relief to such read-
" ers as are not fond of distressful events, and
" melancholy scenes."

Anecdotes of a Convent, by the same Author, and merits the same rank and plaudit.

Soph.

Soph. It is indeed a moſt agreeable book, and the Reviewers have done it juſtice.--I think you have not yet mentioned Mrs. *Griffith*'s Novels.

Euph. Mrs. *Griffith*'s Novels are moral and ſentimental, though they do not riſe to the firſt claſs of excellence, they may fairly be ranked in the ſecond, they are very unexceptionable and entertaining books.—Their Titles are:—*The Delicate Diſtreſs.*—*The Gordian Knot* (by Mr. G.)—*Lady Barton*—*Lady Juliana Harley*—Mr. and Mrs. G. are well known as the Authors of the ingenious *Letters of Henry and Frances,* and ſome other pieces of merit.

Hort. I have ſeen a book called, *Letters from Altamont in Town to his Friends in the Country,* which in my opinion has great merit.

Euph. Indiſputably.—It was written by Mr. *Jenner,* Author of the *Placid Ma:,* of whom I ſhall have occaſion to ſay more, when we come to our moral inferences.

The Hiſtory of Charles Wentworth, Eſq; is a work of Genius and Originality, but it is not proper for all readers, it is ſtrongly tinctured with Deiſm, and is evidently written in

favour

favour of that uncomfortable Syſtem, and like *Rouſſeau,* he appeals to ſavages in confirmation of his tenets, it is therefore an improper book for youth.

The Man of Feeling—and the *Man of the World,* are by the ſame Author, Mr. *Mackenzie.*—both are moral, natural, and pathetic, aud worthy of our plaudit; if there is any defect, is is that ſome of the ſcenes are ſhocking repreſentations of human nature, and bear too hard upon the readers humanity and ſenſibility.

Soph. Pray what is your opinion of Miſs *Minifie's* Novels?

Euph They are in the claſs of mediocrity, if I were to mention ſuch, it would make our taſk too long and tedious, I muſt therefore paſs over theſe, and hundreds beſide that are very innocent and moral books.

Soph. I ſaw a book upon your ſhelf called, *The Portrait of Life, in a Series of Novels.*

Euph. It is only a compilation from different Authors, a common and eaſy method of book-making in theſe days: there are a
great

great number of thefe publications, and it is
furprizing they fhould anfwer to the trade.—
The pleafing Inftructor—*The entertaining No-
velift*—*Old Heads upon young Shoulders,* &c.
—*ad infinitum.*——Thefe compilations are
fhameful impofitions upon the public, and
ought to be difcouraged by every citizen of
the Republic of Letters; the moft effectual
method would be to enter every book that is
worthy of publication at Stationers Hall.

Hort. Is it not equally injurious to Authors,
to publifh extracts of books in Magazines
and other periodical publications?

Euph. Certainly.—And unlefs I am miftaken, the method I propofe would put an
end to thefe pilfering practices, for they deferve to be called fo.

Soph. I have feen a Novel called *Conftan-
tia, or the diftreffed Friend,* which I think is
above the common place Novels of the circulating library.

Euph. You have given it the place it deferves, below excellence and above contempt.

Louifa

Louisa a sentimental Novel, may be ranked a step higher, but not on the first form.—It is of the melancholy kind.—There are a great number of Novels of the same class, and we might fill a volume with a list of them: but we are now come to a resting place,—I have brought my work down to a later period than I at first intended; it is time to draw towards a conclusion.

Hort. I hope you are not serious?—Your plan is by no means compleated.

Euph. I am very sensible that it is not, but this part of it is.—For what remains to be said I have more reason to fear it will be too much, than too little.—I shall endeavour to draw it into a small a compass as possible, with your assistance.—For this time we must adjourn.

Hort. I shall have many questions to ask, and perhaps some objections to make; I think also there are many books omitted.

Euph. At our next meeting I will hear and answer all your demands, if I do not, (as I have already done,) anticipate your objections.

jections.—I shall bring with me a list of Novels Original and uncommon.—I shall speak of Tales and Fables out of the reach of nature, though not of Criticism: and having dispatched these, we will gather up the clue of our progress, and proceed to inferences.

Soph. I rejoice to hear that you are not come to a final conclusion. I hope to see you at my house next Thursday.

Hort. I will not fail you.—I perceive that *Euphrasia* has yet much to say.—Perhaps I may be of some service, in protracting the conclusion you apprehend.

Euph. Don't frighten me *Hortensius*.—I wish rather to contract than extend my plan, as I shall shew you at our next meeting.

Hort. I take my leave for this Evening Ladies.

EVENING

EVENING XI.

Hortenſius, Sophronia, Euphraſia.

Hort. EVER ſince our laſt meeting I have been reflecting upon ſeveral things you ſaid at that time; and I beg leave to make ſome remarks.

Euph. I will hear them moſt willingly, and endeavour to profit by them.

Hort. You excepted againſt compilations very juſtly, and you adviſed a method to prevent them. You wiſhed to prevent long extracts of books being inſerted in periodical publications:—did you mean that this prohibition ſhould extend to the Reviewers?

Euph. By no means.—As the Cenſors of literature they ought to have an excluſive right to give extracts of every publication
that

that deferves their recommendation: but I could wifh this fovereign power were re-ftrained within certain bounds.

Hort. In what refpect?—You muft depend upon their judgement and candour.

Euph. Certainly;—and you may appeal from their Sentence to the public at large.— I wifh they could confine and limit their extracts to the compafs of one *Monthly Review*; for it is not fair to fkim off the cream of an Author's dairy, and leave only the dregs behind: or in other words, to gratify the reader's curiofity, and prevent his pur-chafing the book; and thus intercepting the reward of the Author's labours, which I be-lieve happens requently.

Hort. What you now fay is very juft, you would leave them perfectly free and unre-ftrained in their judgement, and only limit their extracts.

Euph. That is my wifh in favour of all writers; whofe property in their own works is already too much abridged by an arbitrary

D 2   decifion

decifion of power, over literature and her off-
fpring.

Soph. Thefe remarks lead us from the pro-
fecution of our fubject.

Hort. Not entirely.—I muft afk another
queftion:—why fhould you finifh your progrefs and retrofpect here?—I fee no reafon
why it fhould not be continued down to the
prefent year.

Euph. I gave you my reafons at our Ninth
meeting, and as we come nearer to the prefent time, they grow ftronger.—I have brought
my progrefs down to the clofe of the year
1770, which is juft ten years lower than I at
firft intended.—It would be an invidious tafk
to fpeak of the writers of the prefent day;
let us leave them to the Reviewers, it is their
province.—If they do not all the juftice the
Authors may think they deferve, let them
appeal to the *public*, and to *time*, and truft to
their impartiality, for their fentence will be
juft, and irreverfible.

Hort. You will not then fuffer your late
publications to be mentioned, though they
belong to your proper fubject?

Euph.

Euph. No certainly.—If they deserve to be remembered, I have no doubt they will survive me: and if not, let them be forgotten. —You will now give me leave to read you my list of Novels and Stories Original and uncommon. I have already enlarged upon some of them.

Tale of a Tub.
Gulliver's Travels. } by *Swift.*
Bunyan's Pilgrim's Progress.
Patrick's Pilgrim.
Don Quixote, by *Cervantes.*
Modern Don Quixote, by *Marivaux.*
Robinson Crusoe, by *Defoe.*
Gaudentio di Lucca, by Bishop *Berkeley.*
Peter Wilkins.
Voyage to the Moon.
Chrysal—or *Adventures of a Guinea.*
Reverie—or *flight to the Paradise of Fools.*
Arsaces, Prince of Betlis.

These three last by the same Author, and all of the satyrical kind.

Life of John Buncte, Esq.
John Buncle, jun. Esq.

Tristram

Triſtram Shandy, Gent.

Life and Adventures of Common Senſe.

Citizen of the World.

Pilgrim of China.

The Spiritual Quixote, an Antidote to Methodiſm.

The Caſtle of Otranto—printed at *Strawberry-Hill.*—I have ſpoken largely of this work in a former publication of mine.

Theſe are all of great merit in their kind, and of moral tendency.

Soph. You abridge now indeed, as you threatened to do.

Euph. It is time that I ſhould bring my progreſs to a period, I have enlarged upon the moſt eminent works of the kind, and have given a general character of thoſe laſt mentioned.

I ſhall next introduce another ſpecies of the ſame Genus of writing, which will make ſome variety in our progreſs.—I will lead you into enchanted palaces,—delicious gardens,—and endleſs labyrinths.—We will put ourſelves under the protection of the good genii,

and

and they will conduct us out of them by an invisible gate, where we shall find ourselves much forwarder, and have in view the place where we shall finish our journey.

Soph. I am pleased with the excursion of your fancy, I hope you will permit us to stop sometimes, and take a view of the curiosities of the places we pass through.

Euph. You must not tarry a long while any where, and there are very few of these places that will bear a close inspection.

Hort. I shall follow you as *Æneas* did the *Sybil,* with the same confidence, that you will guide me through in safety.

Euph. The allusion is not amiss.—Oh that you could realize the golden bough !

Hort. I am afraid the tree does not grow in this country.

Euph. Yes it does, but is guarded by Hesperian dragons, and there are a thousand dangers and vexations in the way of those who adventure for the prize.—But this is trifling away time.

D 4

Hort.

Hort. Let us then advance, and may you obtain the golden prize!

Euph. Here is my list and a few notes upon it.

TALES *and* FABLES *ancient and modern.*

You have doubtless read the fables of *Æsop, Pilpay,* and *Locman*—and imitations of them without end.—There is an opinion lately gone forth, that fables are improper for children. I shall not now investigate this subject, but it does not appear to me that those ages that were instructed by Fable and Allegory, were less virtuous than the present times are; and this *Criterion* will apply to many other kinds of writing besides that before us.

Hort. This is taking a short way of deciding an important question.

Euph. If it be a *certain* one, the shorter the better; if not it shall give place to a better.—Will you be the person to give it?

Hort. Not in this place,—it would interfere with our present business,—we will postpone the subject for the present, and beg of you to proceed with your allegorical fables.

Euph.

Euph. I do not presume to assert that they are absolutely the best, or the only method of instruction, but that they do not deserve to be despised or exploded.

> Who spoke in *Parables* I need not say;—
> But sure he knew it was a pleasant way,
> Sound sense by plain examples to convey. DRYDEN.

There are many works of this kind, that are excellent and instructive, both in prose and verse.—I will mention briefly, *Gay's Fables,*— *Cotton's Visions,*—*Moore's Fables for the Female Sex, &c.*—But it requires a skilful hand to select books of this kind for youth, because there are many professedly written for this purpose that are very improper; and if books for youth are ill chosen they will do more harm than good. *Mr. Dodsley's Collection of Fables ancient and modern,* is the best that I know.

Hort. I agree with you in this point, and indeed in most others; and when I seem to oppose you, it is only to give you a *fillup,* and to make you exert yourself.—Nevertheless, I intend to have another contest with you before

I

I quit the field.—In the mean time I beg you
to proceed.

Euph. Let us then take a brief ſurvey of
Eaſtern Tales, a claſs of ſo ſmall extent. I have
ſpoken largely of the *Arabian Nights Entertainment* as a work of Originality and Authenticity, and let me add of amuſement.
The great demand for this book, raiſed a
ſwarm of imitations, moſt of which are of
the French manufactory, as the *Perſian Tales
—Turkiſh Tales—Tartarian Tales—Chineſe
Tales—Peruvian Tales—Mogul Tales—&c.*

The ſtories of this kind are all wild and extravagant to the higheſt degree; they are indeed ſo far out of the bounds of Nature and
probability, that it is difficult to judge of
them by rules drawn from theſe ſources.—It
cannot be denied that ſome of them are amuſ-
ing, and catch hold of the readers attention.

Soph. They do more than catch the attention, for they retain it.—There is a kind of
faſcination in them,—when once we begin a
volume, we cannot lay it aſide, but drive
through

through to the end of it, and yet upon re-flexion we defpife and reject them.

Hort. They are certainly dangerous books for youth,—they create and encourage the wildeft excurfions of imagination, which it is, or ought to be, the care of parents and precep-tors to reftrain, and to give them a juft and true reprefentation of human nature, and of the duties and practice of common life.

Euph. You fpeak as if it was the general ftudy of parents and teachers in our days to educate our youth to wifdom and virtue.—Is it not their ambition to make them know-ing rather than wife, and fafhionable rather than virtuous?—thus they are hackney'd in the ways of the world, and though ignorant of every thing that is really good and efti-mable, they are *old* before their days are half fpent.

Soph. The books that are put into the hands of youth, do in a great meafure direct their purfuits and determine their characters; it is therefore of the firft confequence that they fhould be well chofen.—After the cha-

racter

racter is formed, books of entertainment
may be recommended, and read with safety,
and sometimes with advantage.

Hort. You do not mean to recommend any
of the books last named?

Euph. I do not; and yet it will be well if
youngpeople read nothing worse.—The *Eastern Tales* have raised a vast number of imitations, and many readers are extremely fond
of them.—Madame *D'Anois* was a famous
composer of *Fairy Tales,*—she likewise wrote
a Romance called *Hyppolitus Earl of Doug-
las,* which had then, and even now has its admirers, though it is as wild and improbable
as the *Fairy Tales,* or *Eastern Fables.*—The
Count de Gabalis may be reckoned among
these excursions of a raised imagination.

I shall read you a list of some more modern
works of the same kind.

Rasselas, Prince of Abissinia—Dr. *Johnson.*
Almoran and Hamet—*Hawkesworth.*
Soliman and Almena—*Langhorne*
Nourjahad—Mrs. *Sheridan.*
Mirza and Fatima, an Indian Tale.

Tales

Tales of the Genii.

The Perſian Tales of Inatulla.

Miſcellany of Eaſtern Learning.

Chineſe Anecdotes.

Leſſings Fables.

Abaſſai, an Eaſtern Story.

Loves of Othniel and Achſah.—I do not pretend to give an opinion whether this ſtrange book be ancient or modern, but there is reaſon to think it was written by a Jew.

The Triumph of Reaſon over Fancy—a fanciful ſtory.

The Viſiers,—or *enchanted Labyrinth*—of the ſame kind.

There are many other books of this claſs, but theſe are all within my knowlege that are worthy of mention.

There would be no end of reciting the names of theſe Tales.

Hort. There is ſomething very pleaſing in *Eaſtern Stories* well told. There was a paſſion at all times for ſtory-telling in all the countries beyond the Levant.—I remember an incident in a book of travels that is a proof of the continuance of this cuſtom.

The

The traveller had engaged himfelf to make a journey into Upper Egypt, without the knowledge and confent of his friends, in fearch of antiquities, and to carry on a traffic privately for precious ftones.—The dangerous circumftances attending this negociation, and the other hazards he run of perifhing in a barbarous country, affected his mind and difturbed his reft; he confeffed to his friend and patron, that he fuffered much from his inward agitations.   His patron rallied him upon his want of refolution, and afked him if he had not yet learned the Turkifh method of calming his mind?—The traveller thought he meant the ufe of opium or fome drug of that kind, but he foon after called for a young man his fervant, and ordered him to take up a book and read where he left off the night before,—the youth did as he was directed, and read a very pleafant ftory, to which the traveller was attentive, and found his mind relieved and comforted.—When the lad had done reading, his mafter raifed many queftions,

and

and made remarks upon the story, and then spoke to his guest as follows:—" You see my friend, that we are not such Barbarians as many of the Franks believe us,—your people are extremely vain and conceited of their own customs, and yet provoked to see others tenacious of theirs; they laugh at our Turkish stories, and at this method of soothing our cares; yet I conceive that it is as natural and as innocent as gaming, or drinking great quantities of wine, which are your common diversions."—The traveller could not help admitting the truth of what he said, and observed, that it was strange that writers of Travels should censure the Turks and Moors for their passion for hearing Tales and Stories, when at the same time if this inclination did not prevail among Christians, their books could not be read at all."

Euph. We are much obliged for your Story, which illustrates our subject,—I will produce another of the same kind. M. *de Guys* in his *Sentimental Journey through Greece*, takes notice of the same passion for tales and stories.

ftories.—When a party of women met together they frequently entertained each other
with telling a ftory in turn, which amufement is called *Paramythia*.—He defcribes
fome young girls at their needle-work, one of
them fays, "Come, let us have a party at
the *Paramythia*, thefe pretty amufements will
lighten our work.—I will tell you the fine
Perfian ftory my father taught me."

Soph. In fhort the paffion for tales and ftories is common to all times, and all countries, and varies only according to the cuf-
toms and manners of different people ; and
thofe who moft affect to defpife them under
one form, will receive and admire them in
another.

Euph. Nothing is more true, it is the felection of them, that makes them an innocent or a pernicious amufement.

I have now done with *Eaftern Tale*s and
Stories.

Hort. May I then afk a queftion or two?

Euph. As many as you pleafe.—We are
now at a proper refting place.

Hort.

Hort. What is your opinion of *Ossian*'s works, and the *Erse* poetry?

Euph. You could not have asked me a more difficult question. I read Dr. *Johnson*'s sentiments on this head, and was satisfied with his decision: but I have since read Mr. *Mc Nichol*'s *Remarks upon Johnson's Tour,* and that overset all that the Doctor had said. There is something imperious and dogmatical in his manner of criticizing, and in the present case he seems to have wanted both judgment and candour.—On the other hand, *Mc Nichol* shews too much of bitterness and acrimony, and of the same national pride as he condemns in *Johnson,* but he appeals to facts and to living persons of character and veracity, and such evidence is not easily set aside.

Hort. I wish you would leave Dr. *Johnson* and Mr. *Mc Nichol* to settle their disputes between themselves, and give us your own opinion.

Euph. I ought first to shew you the grounds of my opinion, and to do that I must relate another curious circumstance.

A friend of mine wrote to a young gentleman who was in the Highlands, obferving
the remains of Antiquity there, and making
enquiry into the authenticity of *Offian*'s works.
My friend fent the traveller a fragment of
his own compofing, in imitation of *Offian*'s
manner—He fhewed it to feveral perfons in
the Highlands, and afked what they thought
of it?—they told him it was one of *Offian*'s
fragments, and they remembered it perfectly
well.—This proof of difingenuity in fupport
of the national claim to *Offian*'s credit, ren-
ders very doubtful every account we receive
from the natives of his country.

Hort. This is indeed a curious circumftance.—but I want to have your opinion
upon this complicated evidence.

Euph. You oblige me to go farther into
many fubjects than I intended, and you muft
bear whatever blame I fhall incur. I believe
that Mr. *Macpherfon* collected together all
the traditional ftories of the Highlands, that
he put them into his own loom, and wove
them into a regular piece.

His

His works bear ſtrong marks of genius and Originality, they are bold and figurative, and ſome of them are highly pleaſing. It is certainly a very reſpectable collection.—The ingenious and unfortunate *Chatterton*'s compoſitions I think to be of the ſame kind.—The ground-work his Manuſcripts, the building his own.

Hort. In what claſs of writing would you place *Oſſian*,—pray tell us?—In the Romance or Novel?—or will you give him a place among your Epic Poets?

Euph. It is difficult to aſſign a place to the writings of *Oſſian*.—*Fingal* is undoubtedly an Epic, but not a Poem.—I cannot give that name to what is neither proſe nor verſe, —this ſort of writing, corrupts and ſpoils our language, and deſtroys the barrier, which nature has placed, to diſtinguiſh between poetry and proſe.—I think if you have no objection I would reckon *Oſſian* among the Romances.

Hort. With all my heart, I give him up to your ſentence.—But I do not feel myſelf ſatisfied with your treatment of the great Epic

E 2   Poets

Poets *Homer* and *Virgil*, whofe works you have as I think degraded, by bafe comparifons.—Thofe who are placed at the top of *Parnaffus*.

Euph. And think you there are no other Epic poets but *Homer* and *Virgil* ?

Hort. None worthy to be placed in the firft rank of excellence.

Euph. I fuppofe there may have been many, but fome are loft by time and accident. I have mentioned the *Knight*'s *Tale* in *Chaucer*, the *'Squire*'s *Tale* is of the fame kind.— Many of the metrical Romances ought to be ranked as Epic poems.—And will you deny the title of Epic poets to *Ariofto* ?—To *Taffo* ?—To *Guarini* ?—To *Camoens* ?—To *Milton* ?

Hort. I do not.—But I look upon them as only fuccefsful imitators of the great Ancients.

Euph. You put me in mind of a prejudice I received in my youth, from reading the verfes placed before the firft editions of *Milton*.

Three

Three poets in three diftant ages born,
Greece, Italy, and England did adorn,
The firft in loftinefs of thought furpafs'd,—
The next in Majefty,—in both the laft.—
The force of nature, could no farther go,
To make a third fhe join'd the former two.

I underftood this compliment literally,
and believed there never were but three Epic
poets, and that it was impoffible there could
ever be a fourth.

Hort. And you think I have a prejudice of
the fame kind?—According to your account,
Epic poets are as plentiful as mufhrooms.

Euph. Not fo neither—they are rare, but
not fo fcarce as is generally believed.—*Pope*
had laid a plan for an Epic Poem that might
have equalled him to your great Ancients.

Hort. I hope you reckon Sir *Richard Blackmore* in your lift of Epic poets?

Euph It is not a man's believing himfelf a
poet, that will oblige the world to receive him
as fuch :—many other writers have been under the fame miftake as *Blackmore*.—If we
leave it to time to decide the point, it will ap-

E 3   pear

pear which is the real, and which the pretended Genius.

Hort. But will you make no amends for your heretical opinions of *Homer* and *Virgil?*

Euph. I have no amends to make.—I have placed them at the head of their class, and paid them every mark of respect and veneration.

Hort. Then we have only traced the circle, and returned to the same place we set out from.

Soph. And there let us rest, and leave time also to decide upon it. I have waited some time to mention some books that *Euphrasia* has either pass'd by, or reserved for her last class:—I mean the German Stories,—or what will you call them, of *Gesner, Klopstock,* and other writers, or paraphrasers of the Scripture stories?

Euph. I cannot say I am an admirer of them.—I have already spoken against all those stories where truth and fiction are blended together.—If this is exceptionable in profane History, it is certainly much more so in regard

gard to Scripture.—The tranſlations of theſe books help to ſpoil our language, which has ſuffered much by ſuch innovations, and much more from paltry imitations of them. I wiſh they were all laid on an heap, and burnt together.

Hort. I knew a worthy divine of our church, who expreſſed the ſame wiſh, reſpecting all the commentaries on the Scriptures, and ſaid that men would be the better Chriſtians for it.

Euph. I do not preſume to give an opinion upon ſo important a ſubject, but I do think there are too many books upon moſt others. It is perhaps providential that ſome ſhould be forgotten, to make room for others, or elſe literally the world would not contain them.

Soph. I have ſeen a book called the *Hiſtory of Joſeph*, of the kind I mentioned. It was attributed to Mrs. *Rowe*, of whoſe writings you have made no mention.

Euph. Mrs. *Rowe*'s writings are very reſpectable.—They breathe a true ſpirit of piety, tinctured with a degree of Enthuſiaſm, above the reach of ordinary Chriſtians.

E 4 Her

Her *Letters moral and entertaining*, are very proper for youth.

She wrote a poem, called *Joseph*, which is not unworthy of a place upon the ſhelf with other modern Epic poems.—One of the admirers of the German books above named, has paraphraſed Mrs. *Rowe*'s *Joseph*, and extended it to a thick Octavo volume; and put it into the ſame kind of language, which is neither proſe nor verſe. It grieves me to ſee this traſh circulate while the poem is forgot.

The German books of this kind are:
The *Death of Abel*, by *M. Geſner*.
The *Meſſiah*, by *M. Klopſtock*.
Noah,
I ſhall not mention the Engliſh imitations, but leave them quietly to their repoſe.

I have now done with this neutral claſs of writing, and with all the reſt of the Genus. What remains is to conſider the effects of Novel reading upon the manners, and to draw ſome inferences, with an humble view to public utility.—But this muſt be the ſubject of a future converſation, for it grows late.

Soph.

Soph. You have brought us, as you threatened, within view of our journey's end.

Euph. If I have omitted any works of eminence, I ſhall be glad to be reminded of it before I conclude.   It is very probable that I may.

Hort. If you have it is very excuſable in ſo numerous a claſs of writers.   I think you have done juſtice to every body, but the Ancient Poets.

Euph. Who ſhall decide this point for us both?—Will you give conſent that I ſhould appeal to the Public to decide upon it?

Hort. In what manner will you aſk the public opinion?

Euph. Be it known to you, that I have written down all our converſations as ſoon as I left you, and got into my own cloſet.— But I will keep my word, and not publiſh the work without your conſent.

Hort. It is a point of ſome conſequence. —I will conſider of it, and tell you the reſult at our next meeting.

Soph.

Soph. I shall wait for your decision, before I give my own;—in the interval I shall beg permission to read *Euphrasia*'s manuscript.

Euph. With all my heart.   You have both a right to see it, consider it well, and decide its fate.—For this time I take my leave.

Hort. It is time that you should have some respite.—Pray let us know when you are at leisure to finish this subject.

Euph. I will send you word when I am prepared to receive you.

Hort. Ladies, a good evening to you both !

EVENING

EVENING XII.

Hortenſius, Sophronia, Euphraſia.

Hort. LADIES well met!— this clear froſty day has tempted you to walk.

Euph. Sophronia tempted me abroad, out of regard for my health.

Soph. I did indeed, for ſedentary amuſe-ments, have hurt both her health and ſpirits. There is no way of enduring the cold but by bidding it defiance,—exerciſe renews our health and ſpirits.

Hort. I rejoice to find you purſuing this ſa-lutary maxim,—no people are born too ten-der to endure their own climate,—it is in-dulgence and luxury that effeminates us, and then we complain of our country, and fly to

others

others to recover what we have loſt by our own fault.

Soph. Britain was always eſteem'd a mild and temperate country till within the laſt century.

Hort. You ſay true, and the preſent race are not very like the deſcendants of the Britons that were found here by *Julius Cæſar*.

Euph. The Britons are not more altered in this, than in all other reſpects—their manners,—their cuſtoms,—their amuſements.

Hort. Their amuſements will bring us to our old ſubject,—ſuppoſe you both go home with me, and purſue it there?

Euph. No—It is you that muſt go with me, my notes and extracts are in my own library, and I ſhall want them frequently.

Hort. I am ready to attend you at this time, but the next viſit muſt be to me.

Euph. We ſhall then have concluded our progreſs, and I ſhall aſk your advice in regard to a future undertaking.

Hort. At your pleaſure,—but do not ſhorten your walk.

Soph.

Soph. She is glad of a pretence to finish it I assure you.

Euph. I will not reply to the charge.—*Hortensius* you shall say all that you can against Novels,—I will reply to your censures, and *Sophronia* shall be Moderator between us.

Hort. I shall not spare them, notwithstanding the ill success I have had whenever I have been your opponent.

Euph. Nor shall I contradict you, unless when your censure is too general and indiscriminate, on works of Genius, taste, and morality.

Soph. It is no easy task to separate and select them, for they are found altogether, good, bad, and indifferent, in the Chaos of a circulating Library.

Euph. A Circulating Library is indeed a great evil,—young people are allowed to subscribe to them, and to read indiscriminately all they contain; and thus both food and poison are conveyed to the young mind together.

Hort. I should suppose that if books of the worst kind were excluded; still there would be
enough

enough to lay a foundation of idleneſs and folly —A perſon uſed to this kind of reading will be diſguſted with every thing ſerious or ſolid, as a weakened and depraved ſtomach rejects plain and wholſome food.

Soph. There is truth and juſtice in your obſervation,—but how to prevent it?

Hort. There are yet more and greater evils behind.—The ſeeds of vice and folly are ſown in the heart,—the paſſions are awakened,—falſe expectations are raiſed.—A young woman is taught to expect adventures and intrigues,—ſhe expects to be addreſſed in the ſtyle of theſe books, with the language of flattery and adulation.—If a plain man addreſſes her in rational terms and pays her the greateſt of compliments,—that of deſiring to ſpend his life with her,—that is not ſufficient, her vanity is diſappointed, ſhe expects to meet a Hero in Romance.

Euph. No *Hortenſius*,—not a Hero in Romance, but a fine Gentleman in a Novel:—you will not make the diſtinction.

Hort.

Hort. I aſk your pardon, I agreed to the diſtinction and therefore ought to obſerve it.

Euph. I would not have interrupted you on this punctilio; but let us walk into the houſe, and purſue the ſubject in the Library.

Hort. Now you are armed with your extracts, you think yourſelf invulnerable.

Euph. I will not attempt to contradict you, unleſs I have good reaſon for it.—I beg you to proceed with your remarks.

Hort. From this kind of reading, young people fancy themſelves capable of judging of men and manners, and that they are knowing, while involved in the profoundeſt ignorance. They believe themſelves wiſer than their parents and guardians, whom they treat with contempt and ridicule:—Thus armed with ignorance, conceit, and folly, they plunge into the world and its diſſipations, and who can wonder if they become its victims?—For ſuch as the foundation is, ſuch will be the ſuperſtructure.

Euph. All this is undoubtedly true, but at the ſame time would you exclude all works of
fiction

fiction from the young reader?—In this cafe you would deprive him of the pleasure and improvement he might receive from works of genius, taste and morality.

Hort. Yes, I would serve them as the Priest did *Don Quixote's* library, burn the good ones for being found in bad company.

Euph. That is being very severe, especially if you confider how far your execution would extend.—If you would prohibit reading *all* works of fiction, what will become of your favourites the great Ancients, as well as the most ingenious and enlightened modern writers?

Soph. Surely this is carrying the prohibition too far, and though it may found well in Theory, it would be utterly impracticable.

Hort. I do not deny that.—There are many things to be wished, that are not to be hoped. I fee no way to cure this vice of the times, but by extirpating the caufe of it.

Euph. Pray *Hortenfius*, is all this feverity in behalf of our fex or your own?

Hort. Of both.—Yet yours are most concerned in my remonstrance for they read more
of

of thefe books than ours, and confequently
are moft hurt by them.

Euph. You will then become a Knight er-
rant, to combat with the windmills, which
your imagination reprefents as Giants; while
in the mean time you leave a fide unguarded.

Hort. And you have found it out.—Pray
tell me without metaphors, your meaning in
plain Englifh?

Euph. It feems to me that you are unreafon-
ably fevere upon thefe books, which you fuppofe to be appropriated to our fex, (which
however is not the cafe):—not confidering
how many books of worfe tendency, are put
into the hands of the youth of your own,
without fcruple.

Hort. Indeed!—how will you bring proofs
of that affertion?

Euph. I will not go far for them. I will
fetch them from the School books, that generally make a part of the education of young
men.—They are taught the Hiftory—the Mythology—the morals—of the great Ancients,
whom you and all learned men revere,—But

with these, they learn also—their Idolatry—
their follies—their vices—and every thing
that is shocking to virtuous manners.—*Lu-
tretius* teaches them that *fear* first made
Gods—that men grew out of the earth like
trees, and that the indulgence of the passions
and appetites, is the truest wisdom.—*Juvenal*
and *Persius* describe such scenes, as I may
venture to affirm that Romance and Novel-
writers of any credit would blush at:—and
Virgil—the modest and delicate *Virgil*, in-
forms them of many things, they had better
be ignorant of.—As a woman I cannot give
this argument its full weight.—But a hint is
sufficient,—and I presume you will not deny
the truth of my assertion.

Hort. I am astonished—admonished—and
convinced!—I cannot deny the truth of what
you have advanced, I confess that a reformation is indeed wanting in the mode of Education of the youth of our sex.

Soph. Of both sexes you may say.—We
will not condemn yours and justify our own.
—You are convinced, and *Euphrasia* will use
her victory generously I am certain.

Euph.

Euph. You judge rightly.—I do not prefume to condemn indifcriminately, the books
ufed in the education of youth; but furely
they might be better felected, and fome
omitted, without any difadvantage.—I fear
there is little profpect of fuch a general reformation as *Hortenfius* generoufly wifhes for
If any method can be found to alleviate
thefe evils, it muft be lenient—gradual—and
practicable.—Let us then try to find out fome
expedient, with refpect to thofe kind of
books, which are our proper fubject.

As this kind of reading is fo common, and
fo much in every body's power, it is the more
incumbent on parents and guardians to give
young people a good tafte for reading, and
above all to lay the foundation of good principles from their very infancy; to make them
read what is really good, and by forming
their tafte teach them to defpife paltry books
of every kind.—When they come to maturity
of reafon, they will fcorn to run over a circulating Library, but will naturally afpire to
read the beft books of all kinds.

Soph

Soph. In moſt caſes it would ſuperſede the evil we complain of: but for the middling and lower ranks of people, I apprehend this would not hinder either children or ſervants from reading Novels.

Euph. The beſt way to do this is to find them conſtant employment. In every rank and ſituation, people may ſuperintend the education of their children, and " *train them up in the way they ſhould go.*" There is no duty enjoined but what is practicable.—I am afraid the negligence of parents, is too often the cauſe of a wrong bias in their children,— or elſe their falſe indulgence, which is equally prejudicial to them.

With all theſe precautions in view, I would ſelect ſuch books as were proper to be put into the hands of youth; and with the ſame circumſpection I would carry them to the Theatres, to ſatisfy the curioſity of youth, and prevent their taking theſe amuſements clandeſtinely, for how in an age like this, cou'd I flatter myſelf I cou'd prevent them ?

Soph.

Soph. This is indeed the medium between the two extremes, and I think *Hortenſius* can make no objection to it.

Hort. I can only ſay that were I a father, I would ſuffer no ſuch books to come into my houſe.

Euph. Then your children would borrow them of their young friends,—indeed *Hortenſius* your prohibition would be to no purpoſe.

Hort. Then I thank GOD I am not in a ſituation to want to uſe it !

Euph. You do not conſider that there are ſome works of this kind to which you have given your plaudit, and others, which I have ſhewn you were written as an antidote to the bad effects of them tho' under the diſguiſe and name of Novels.

Hort. Well, that is true, and I will allow that when the principles are fixed, and the character formed, they may be read with ſafety , but that there are very few of them proper for youth to read: and as there are upon a moderate calculation ten of the wrong ſort to one of the right, it is ten to one that a child meets with the former.

Soph. You are now more candid and rea-
fonable, and we will agree with you. But
Euphrafia is looking over her extracts, fhe
has more to fay to you.

Euph. I have faid that there are a kind of
books, which tho' publifhed under the title
of Novels, are defigned as an antidote to the
bad effects of them. I have fome Extracts
from thefe, which I hope you will think worthy of your attention.

But firft I fhall give you an Extract from
*A Comparative View of the State and Facul-
ties of Man, with thofe of the Animal World,*
by Dr. *Gregory,* a work generally read and
admired.

" Notwithftanding the abfurdities of the
" old Romance, it feems calculated to pro-
" duce more favorable effects on the morals
" of mankind than our modern Novels. If
" the former did not reprefent men as they
" really are, it reprefented them better. Its
" heroes were patterns of courage, truth,
" generofity, humanity, and the moft exalted
" virtues,—its heroines were diftinguifhed
" for

" for modesty, delicacy, and the utmost dig-
" nity of manners. The latter represent man-
" kind too much what they really are, and
" paint such scenes of pleasure and vice as
" are unworthy to see the light, and thus in
" a manner hackney youth in the ways of
" wickedness before they are well entered
" into the world; they expose the fair sex in
" the most wanton and shameless manner to
" the eyes of the whole world, by stripping
" them of that modest reserve, which is the
" foundation of grace and dignity, the veil
" with which nature intended to protect them
" from too familiar an eye, in order to be at
" once the greatest incitement to love, and
" the greatest security to virtue."

Another passage from the same Author.—
" The pleasure we receive from History,
" arises in a great measure from the same
" source with that we receive from Romance,
" it is not a bare recital of facts that gives
" us pleasure, they must be facts that give
" some agitation to the mind, by their being
" important, interesting, or surprising; but

F 4   " these

" thefe events do not frequently recur in
" Hiftory, it is not furprifing, but it is
" fometimes difficult to keep our attention
" awake."

Hort. Unlefs I am greatly miftaken, this
Extract favours my argument more than
yours.

Euph. I give it up to you, fo make your
moft of it; if it fpeaks truth and reafon, I
will give my affent it, though perhaps I may
not agree to the inferences you may draw
from it.

Soph. It favours *Euphrafia*'s argument in
favour of the old Romances, and fpeaks of
the Novels in contraft with them.

Euph. My next Extract is from the *Placid
Man*, againft exhibiting vicious or fhocking
Characters to public view.

" Tho' a good character may not have
" the defigned effect with regard to improv-
" ing the mind of the reader, a bad one will
" always act ftrongly the contrary way. The
" goodnefs of the one is eafily forgotten,
" but the vicioufnefs of the other cleaves to
                                    " the

" the mind of the young reader, and has its
" effect according to the difposition of him
" who receives it; if that is good, the pic-
" ture of vice may carry a degree of difguft
" with it, which may prevent its doing him—
" much harm; but if it happens to be more
" inclined to evil, (which without being
" uncandid, we may, I fear, fuppofe more
" than an equal chance,) vicious images will
" ftrengthen that propenfity, and however
" careful the Author may have been in ren-
" dering ftrict poetical juftice, by making
" punifhment the certain effect of criminal
" indulgence, the ideas of the indulgence
" will remain upon the mind, after thofe
" of the punifhment are effaced.   I am con-
" vinced that the introducing profligate cha-
" racters either into Novels, or upon the
" Stage by way of expofing them to fhame
" and ridicule, is a very dangerous experi-
" ment, efpecially for young minds; for as
" *Swift*'s *Directions to Servants* is faid to
" have made more bad fervants than ever it
" corrected, by teaching them tricks, which
                                    " without

" without his wit they wou'd never have
" found out; so a series of crimes and follies,
" may give an insight into vice, which the
" good moral drawn from them may not
" prevent being put in practice."

Hort. I entirely approve this Author's re-marks, and believe that the shocking stories exhibited to view in the public papers (fre-quently false or misrepresented,) have a bad effect upon young minds;—they familiarize their eyes to scenes of vice and folly, and sometimes to *crimes* of which they would be *ignorant*, and which are the disgrace of hu-man nature.

Soph. I have often thought so, but how is it possible to prevent it?

Hort. The first step is to point it out, for what remains, it must be left to different times and manners, which we may hope will arise in due time; when poverty and distress, shall have made a general reformation both necessary and practicable:—at present our great men are fully employed, in disputing over the spoils of their unhappy and im-

poverished

poverished country. An Englishman cannot behold it without a sigh, nor speak of it but with indignation.

> Oh England, model to thy inward greatness!
> Like little body with a mighty heart;
> What might'st thou do, that wou'd thee honour do
> Were all thy children kind and natural?
>
> SHAKESPEARE.

Euph. Alas there is but too much foundation for your remarks!—But let us hope the best, and be prepared for the worst.—Let me recal you to the subject, by observing that it was an extract from a *Novel* that led you into these deep reflections.—Confess *Hortensius* that a Novel may be a moral production?

Hort. It would be folly to deny it. But how few are such in comparison of those we have unanimously condemned?

Euph. Perhaps there are more of the better sort than you are acquainted with;—I have had the honour to introduce many to your notice and I may yet increase the number.—I should apologize for my next Extract from a Novel of later date than my limited year 1770—but the Extract itself shall be my apology.

Extract

Extract from the *Trial, or the History of Charles Horton, Esq.*

" If you wish in a Novel to inculcate some
" moral truth, to hide a jewel under so thin
" a veil that its brilliancy may be easily dis-
" cerned, there should always be a reference
" to the manners and the time in which it is
" written; there should be the greatest pro-
" bability, carried thro' the whole allegory,
" that your reason may not be shocked, while
" your imagination is pleased. If Novels
" were properly regulated with this design
" always in view, they might become really
" useful to society. A moral lesson other-
" wise dry and tedious in itself, might be
" communicated in a pleasing dress: as a pill
" has its desired effect, tho' wrapped in a
" gold or silver leaf. The more inviting les-
" sons of instruction are made, certainly the
" better; for who are they that read Novels?
" —Not men of learning, for they despise
" them," (*read affect to despise them,*)—" not
" men of business, for they have other em-
" ployments, —not the rich and great, for
                                                      " they

" they have other amufements.—The mid-
" ling rank of people then are the chief if
" not the only readers,"—*(certainty not the*
" only, *for they are the refource of idle peo-*
" *ple of all ranks and degrees among us)*—
" but particularly the young, the volatile,
" the hearts moft fufceptible of all kinds of
" impreffions.—To thefe the chafteft images
" fhould be prefented, for thefe the pureft
" pictures painted and felected.—Vice fhould
" be reprefented as it really is, attended with
" that trouble and confufion that fhould de-
" ter the wandering feet of innocence and
" credulity from treading in her paths; and
" where it is neceffary to give a loofe to in-
" vention, the greateft care fhould be taken,
" not to pafs the line of decency. Novels
" written with this refpect might be made
" fubfervient to the beft and nobleft pur-
" pofes. Were I a defpotic prince, I would
" fooner hang a man that wrote a work of
" direct, or indirect tendency to corrupt the
" morals of youth, than one who committed
" a robbery on the high road. We degenerate,
" we

" we defcend into the depravities of our na-
" ture too foon, and too eafily; we want no
" enticements of this, or any other kind."

Soph. This Extract makes its own apology.—It is in your favour.

Euph. I have felected fuch paffages as
fpeak the language of truth, candour, and
impartiality, without confidering whether they
favoured my own opinions or not.—I find
one more Extract, but thro' inadvertency I
have omitted the name of the book from
whence it is taken.

" The effects of Romance, and true Hif-
" tory upon young minds is not very diffe-
" rent. The great and important duty of a
" writer is, to point out the difference be-
" tween Virtue and Vice, to fhew one re-
" warded, and the other punifhed; for young
" people pay more regard to prefent good,
" than to future recompenfe,—it is by de-
" grees that they underftand, and admit
" with reluctance, thefe wholfome and ne-
" ceffary truths. It is of the utmoft confe-
" quence that thefe diftinctions fhould be
                                    " enforced

" enforced in the strongest manner, that they
" may be excited to copy good, and avoid
" evil actions. The dullest book that ever
" was written with a moral view, is preferable
" to the most witty and elegant where these
" distinctions are overthrown. How dan-
" gerous and destructive is it then to suffer
" young people to read books where Vice is
" palliated and extenuated, and even recom-
" mended under other names,—where forni-
" cation is called gallantry—dissipation plea-
" sure—prodigality generosity—and selfish-
" ness a due regard to one's own interest.—
" What punishment do such men deserve,
" who write with a design to gratify the va-
" nities, the follies, the passions, the vices
" of youth, and furnish them with excuses
" for the most atrocious actions?—The poor
" pilferer who steals to supply his natural
" wants is hanged, and these pernicious mem-
" bers of society, are rewarded for poisoning
" the morals of the rising generation.—How
" weak, how ineffectual are human laws to
" answer their intended purposes; and bad

" at

" at the world is, it would be much worse,
" if it were not for the interpofition of a fu-
" perior law, in cafes which no human one
" can reach."

Hort. This laft Extract is clearly in my
favour, but I refpect too much your candour
and impartiality to make an unfair ufe of it.

Euph. I thank you for this conceffion.——
We are not very different in opinion,——I would
exclude books of bad tendency from the
hands of youth, as ftrongly as yourfelf, but
I would feparate the *grain* from the *chaff*.

Soph. It is now that I may enter upon my
office of Moderator.——*Hortenfius* would prohibit the reading all Novels in order to exclude the bad ones.——*Euphrafia* would make
a feparation in favour of works of Genius,
tafte, and morality; fhe would recommend
fuch methods of preventing the mifchiefs
arifing from novel reading, as are moderate,
prudent, and above all *practicable*.——

The objections to bad books of this fpecies, are equally applicable to all other kinds
of writing,——indecent novels, indecent plays,

effays,

essays, memoirs, dialogues are equally to be
exploded: but it does not follow that all these
kinds of writing are to be extirpated, because
some are bad.—By the same kind of reasoning we might plead for the prohibition of all
kinds of writing; for excellent and unexceptionable works of every species, may be
contrasted with vicious and immoral ones.
All these objections amount to no more than
that bad books are bad things;—but shall
we therefore prohibit reading?

Hort. You have spoken to some purpose.
—I know that mine is an *Utopian* scheme;
and I acknowledge that *Euphrasia*'s is practicable, if parents and guardians would give
due attention to it.

Euph. Then we are agreed at last,—Selection is to be strongly recommended, and good
books to be carefully chosen by all that are
concerned in the education of youth.—In order to make this work of ours of some public utility, I would recommend some that
may properly be given to children even from
their infancy, and as they grow up towards

VOL. II.   G   maturity

maturity :—that is to fay, if my friends think it worthy to be offered to the public.

Hort. Why, if you will do it in your own name I have no objection,—but I fhould not choofe that mine fhould appear in print.

Euph. I will fo difguife it that you fhall not know yourfelf, and *Sophronia* likewife fhall appear in Mafquerade.

Soph. I leave it entirely to you to difpofe of me, in whatever way you think moft proper for your fervice.

Hort. I am thinking, that from your part in our paft converfations, any perfon who did not know you well, would conclude that your principal, if not only ftudy, had been Romances and Novels.

Euph. I am under no concern on that account, it is not of any confequence how much or how little one knows, but the ufe one makes of the knowledge one has acquired.— If like the induftrious bee I have cull'd from various flowers my fhare of Honey, and ftored it in the common Hive, I fhall have performed the duties of a good citizen of the Republic of letters, and I fhall not have lived in vain.

Hort.

Hort. You are entitled to this approbation from your intention,—and further—

Euph. No further I befeech you. If you pay me any compliments, I fhall be obliged to expunge them from my copy.—If my work deferves public approbation, I truft it will meet with it.

Soph. I am concerned that you fhould have limited yourfelf to a year, for I have wifhed you to fpeak of fome books of later date.

Euph. As Novels I cannot, but only as books deferving public honours, on the fcore of public utility.—As fuch I have a defire to mention the works of the Countefs of *Genlis.*—*The Theatre of Education* for young people, an excellent work.—And her other Publications, *Theodore and Adelaide,* and the *Tales of the Caftle,* are a fchool for Parents, Guardians, and Preceptors.—I had rather be the Author of fuch books as thefe, than be reckoned the firft wit of the Age.

Soph. You have done them juftice, but there are fome Novels of merit within the laft ten years.

Euph.

Euph. The public will do them juftice, and time will fhew, whether they owed their fuccefs to intrific merit, or to the caprice of fafhion. I will not be drawn in to fay any thing more of them.

Hort. We will not urge you any further,— you have fully executed the plan you laid down, and we leave the conclufion to you.

Euph. Here then I conclude, and thank you for your affiftance, and the patience with which you have attended me in my progrefs. As foon as I have made out my lift of books, I will return your vifit *Hortenfius*, and defire your opinion upon it.

Hort. I fhall hope for that pleafure foon.— I now take my leave wifhing you the beft reward of your labours, Fame and Profit!

Soph. I join heartily in the fame wifh.

Euph. Every kind of happinefs attend you my good friends!—For what remains, I fhall (without afking the aid of puffing, or the influence of the tide of fafhion,) leave the decifion to an impartial and difcerning public.

THE

THE Author of the *Progress of Romance*, does not presume to direct such Parents and Guardians in the choice of books for youth, as are qualified to select them; but only to offer to those, who have not thought much upon the subject themselves, and those who commit the charge of education to others; a list of such books as may be put into the hands of children with safety, and also with advantage. This list is confined to books in our own language, and is intended chiefly for the female sex. It is certainly the duty of every Mother, to consider seriously, the consequences of suffering children to read all the books that fall in their way indiscriminately. It is also a very bad and too frequent practice, to give them books above their years and understandings, by the reading of which they seem to the partial parent to acquire a prematurity of knowledge; while

G 3   in

in reality, they are far more ignorant, than
those who advance slowly and surely,—whose
understandings are gradually cultivated, without being over loaded,—and whose reason is
assisted gently and carefully, till it attains its
full maturity.

BOOKS FOR CHILDREN.

A Little Spelling-Book for Children.
J. Newberry's Books for Children.
Marshal's Books for Children.
Mrs. Barbauld's Lessons for Children.
*An easy Introduction to the Knowledge of Na-
 ture, and the Study of the Scriptures, by
 Mrs. Trimmer.*
*Sacred History selected from the Scriptures, by
 Mrs. Trimmer.*
Reading made easy—the best Edition.
Fenning's Spelling-Book.
Dodsley's Fables, ancient and modern.
Lessing's Fables,—translated from the German.
Gay's Fables.

Cotton's

Cotton's Visions.

Female Academy, or History of Mrs. Teachum.

Oeconomy of Human Life.

*Madame de Lambert's Advice to a Son and
Daughter.*

Magazin des Enfans,—translated.

Madame Bonne,—translated.

Geography for Children.

History of England,—Question and Answer.

Roman History,—ditto.

Grecian History,—ditto.

BOOKS FOR YOUNG LADIES.

A Father's Instructions, by Dr. Percival.

A Father's Legacy, by Dr. Gregory.

*Mrs. Talbot's Meditations for every Day in
the Week.*

Mrs. Rowe's Letters, Moral and Entertaining.

Mrs. Chapone's Works.

*Mrs. H. More's Sacred Drama's, and Search
after Happiness.*

Moore's

Moore's Fables for the Female Sex.

Galateo, or the Art of Politeness.

The Lady's Preceptor.

The Geographical Grammar.

Lowth's English Grammar.

The Spectator.

The Guardian.

The Adventurer.

Rambler.

The Connoisseur.

Nature Displayed.

Fontenelle's Plurality of Worlds.

Telemachus.

Travels of Cyrus.

Theatre of Education, by Madame Genlis.

Tales of the Castle, by the same.

Richardson's Works.

Fordyce's Sermons to young Woman.

Mason on Self Knowledge.

The Speaker, by Dr. Enfield.

F I N I S.

THE

THE

HISTORY

OF

CHAROBA,

Queen of Ægypt.

TAKEN FROM A

HISTORY OF ANCIENT ÆGYPT,

ACCORDING TO THE

TRADITIONS OF THE ARABIANS.

THE

HISTORY

OF

CHAROBA,

Queen of Ægypt.

*C*HAROBA, was the only daughter and heir of *Totis* king of *Ægypt*; who was likewise called *Pharaon*, and *Pheron*, by other nations.

In the reign of *Totis*, *Abraham* the beloved of GOD came into *Ægypt*; and it is written, that he would have corrupted *Sarah* the wife of *Abraham*, but GOD punished the king, and delivered his servants. Afterwards *Totis* shewed them great respect, and offered them gold and treasures, but they refused them.

them. Then he recommended *Sarah* to his daughter *Charoba*, and defired her to fhew her fome tokens of refpect. *Charoba* was a young and blooming Virgin, handfome, ingenious, and of a generous fpirit, fhe took *Sarah* into her friendfhip, fhewed her all kinds of honour, and fent her many rich prefents.—*Sarah* brought them all to *Abraham*, and afked his advice concerning them; he ordered her to reftore them, and to fay that they had no need of them.—*Sarah* therefore returned them all to *Charoba*, who was furprifed, and acquainted her father with all that had paffed, which increafed his admiration of them; feeing they refufed all thofe things, which others the moft eagerly fought, and ufed every means to obtain. And he faid unto his daughter,—" Thefe are per-
" fons of high eftimation, who are full of
" holinefs and fincerity, and are not cove-
" tous of perifhable goods;—*Charoba* do
" whatever you can to fhew them honour,
" that they may leave their blefling with us
" when they depart our country.

After

After this, *Charoba* gave *Hagar* unto *Sarah*, who was in due time the mother of our father *Ishmael* (GOD's peace be with him!)—*Hagar* was a beatiful young maiden, a Coptefs by nation. When fhe was prefented to *Sarah*, *Charoba* faid—" Behold thy recompence," therefore *Sarah* called her *Agar*.

When *Abraham* had refolved to return out of *Ægypt* into *Syria*, *Charoba* provided many bafkets of provifion of all kinds, with pre-ferved fruits and many excellent things to eat by the way; faying " thefe things are " only for your accommodation by the way, " and not to enrich you."

Sarah told *Abraham* of this, and he per-mitted her to accept this prefent, faying, " there was no harm in receiving it from " the generous princefs." *Totis* requefted of *Abraham* that he would pray to GOD for his benediction of his country.—*Abraham* there-fore prayed to GOD for *Ægypt* and its inha-bitants.—He alfo gave his benediction to the *Nile*, and told *Totis* that his family fhould reign there for many ages.—Likewife he gave

his

his benediction to *Charoba*, and *Sarah* gave
her the hand of friendfhip, and they departed
out of *Ægypt.*

Charoba caufed mules to be loaden with
her provifions, and fent her own people to
conduct them till they were gotten quite out
of *Ægypt.*

Being got a good way on their journey,
Abraham faid unto *Sarah*, " Give us to eat
" fome of thofe provifions which the princefs
" of *Ægypt* gave unto you." Then *Sarah*
ordered the bafkets to be fet before them,
and they, and their companions alfo, eat of
the provifions.—And they did fo many days.
—But when they came to the laft bafket, they
found it full of precious jewels, and curious
things, and changes of garments.—Where-
upon *Abraham* faid, " this princefs hath de-
" ceived us, and obliged us to accept of her
" treafures.—Great GOD give her fubtilty to
" deceive her enemies, and to vanquifh all
" thofe who fhall arife to do her harm, and
" to ftrive with her for her land!—Blefs her
" in her country, and in her river, and make
                                    " that

" that country a place of plenty, fafety, and
" profperity ! "

When the beloved of GOD was come into
the land of *Syria*, he fpent thofe gifts in
pious works,—in lodging and feeding pil-
grims, and in making many wells, which he
ordered to be common. He alfo bought
flocks and herds, which he fet apart for all
travellers,—for the poor and needy,—for the
lame and the blind : and GOD gave him his
benediction, and caufed his riches to increafe
and multiply. Alfo GOD gave him children
after a long time, and in his old age:—firft
Hagar bore him a fon which was our father
Ifhmael; and after fome years *Sarah* likewife
bare a fon.—And *Hagar* and her fon left *Syria*
and went into *Arabia*.—And *Hagar* fent a
meffenger to *Charoba*, to acquaint her that
fhe had borne a fon,—whereat *Charoba* re-
joiced, and fent her abundance of gold, and
jewels, and fine *Ægyptian* linen, to drefs her
fon withal. Out of thefe treafures *Hagar*
provided ornaments for the fquare temple at
Mecca, and fhe alfo eftablifhed a porter in
the fame temple.

Totis

Totis king of *Ægypt*, lived till after that time, and *Hagar* fent him word that fhe had a ftrong and valiant fon; but that they lived in a barren land, and prayed him to fupply them with provifions.

To this end, *Totis* caufed a channel to be made on the Eaftern fide of *Ægypt*, and brought into it the water of the *Nile*, fo that it carried veffels into the falt fea, which is the channel of the red Sea.—By this way he caufed Wheat to be fent to *Hagar* and her fon, and many other prefents.—They went by water as far as *Gedde*, and from thence were carried to *Mecca* on the backs of beafts. —By thefe means God preferved the inhabitants of *Mecca*, and relieved their wants; —therefore the *Arabians* fpoke well of *Totis*, and called him the *juft*, as having performed the promifes he made them, and given proofs of his good will to them.—Neverthelefs, *Totis* was more feared than beloved in his own Country, for he did many unjuft and cruel actions. Moreover he put many people to death, and particularly thofe of his own family.

family, even his neareſt relations; and this
ke did out of jealouſy of them, leſt they
ſhould deprive his daughter of the crown after his death:—but *Charoba* was of a mild
and gentle diſpoſition, always endeavouring
to prevent the ſhedding of blood. She was
alſo of a great capacity and ingenuity:—ſhe
concealed a near kinſman from the King's
cruelty, and preſerved him and his family;
one of which ſhe afterwards appointed to ſuc-
ceed her on the throne, as we ſhall ſhew hereafter.

Totis in his old age, was hated and feared
by all the nobility; and even *Charoba* dread-
ed his cruelty. She alſo ſuſpected that they
would take away the Crown from his poſterity; therefore, it was ſurmiſed, that ſhe con-
nived at the conſpiracy againſt his life; for
he was poiſoned, but no man knew by what
means, or by what perſons.

After *Totis* was dead, the people could not,
at firſt, agree about a ſucceſſor :—Some ſaid
they would have the race of *Abribus*, one of
their ancient princes,—others would have a

new family called to the throne:—moſt of
them objected to the government of a woman.—While they were thus undetermined,
one of the Viziers roſe up, and ſpoke thus to
them.

"My friends,—*Charoba* is a woman of
"great underſtanding, ſhe is likewiſe of a
"mild and merciful diſpoſition;—there is no
"reaſon why ſhe ſhould be excluded from
"the ſucceſſion:—moreover the good man
"that came from *Syria* and his wife have
"given her their benedictions:—ſhe is be-
"loved by all that are acquainted with her
"noble qualities, and if you take the crown
"from her and give it to another, you will
"certainly have cauſe to repent of your pre-
"cipitation."

The people on better conſideration, inclined to this good advice, and the grandees of
the kingdom by degrees came into it: ſo they
deputed this Vizier to go to *Charoba*, and in
their name, intreat her to fill the vacant
throne. So that Vizier placed *Charoba*, in
the royal ſeat.—The firſt time ſhe ſate on tho
royal

royal throne, she gave great sums away to the people; shewing great liberality, and promising much happiness to all her subjects,—she doubled the pay of the soldiers,—she honoured the priests and sages, and the chiefs of the nobility.—She likewise countenanced the magicians and their fraternity,—she caused the temples to be repaired and enlarged, and built many public edifices. She reigned many years wisely and happily; and she remembered the benediction of *Abraham*, and believed that by the protection of his GOD, she subdued all her enemies, and was respected by her people.

After a long time, it happened that *Gebirus* the *Metaphequian* heard of her fame; and he was minded to pay her a visit, and oblige her to marry him.—*Gebirus* was of a gigantic stature, and descended from the race of the *Gadites*,—and when he sat on the ground seemed as high as the tallest men,—he was strong of body, and fierce of disposition,—he had a distemper in his body that gave him constant pain;—his physicians advised him to seek out another country, the

H 2   soil

foil of which, with the air and water were more
suitable to his temperament.

They gave him such an account of the land of
Ægypt, that he resolved to go and take up his
abode there.—He called together all his people,—he distributed money and arms among
them, and then declared to them his design of
taking possession of the land of *Ægypt*; and
flattered them with the hopes of victory, reward, and a settlement, in a country that was
the garden of the world.—Soon after he began his march, and took with him five
thousand *Gadites*, men of great stature and
strength; every one of which carried a large
stone upon his head, and was completely armed. He travelled till he came to the borders of
Ægypt, and then sent a message to the Queen,
desiring to know in what place she chose
he should enter *Ægypt*; for he was unwilling
to oppose her in any thing, but would appear
to be obedient to all her commands.—His design was to marry her, and make himself King
of *Ægypt*; or, in case she refused him, to dam
up the course of the *Nile*, with the stones his
people

people brought upon their heads,—to turn the
channel into another country and so make the
Ægyptians die of famine, and to ruin their
country. He sent a splendid Embassy to *Charoba*, bragging of his strength and riches,
and offering himself to be her husband.

Charoba had a woman servant, who had
been her nurse,—an artful, subtle, contriving
woman, and a great Enchantress.—*Charoba*
consulted her in all affairs, and advised with
her on this emergency.—She gave her advice
to this effect.—" It seems to me that there is
" no probability of defeating these huge bo-
" dies by fighting, we must rather subdue
" them by stratagem: And to this end, we
" must manage our business so, that they may
" neither do harm to you, nor your sub-
" jects.—I will therefore, with your permis-
" sion, go myself to him and give an answer
" to his embassy in your name."

The Queen bade her do what seemed best
to her. She ordered many of her servants
to wait upon the nurse, to do her honour in

H 3   the

the fight of the Prince, and to fhew that fhe was highly efteemed by her miftrefs.

The nurfe took with her, prefents of the moft valuable things in *Ægypt*,—precious ftones, carved works, preferved fruits, coftly garments, perfumes, arms, fine tempered fwords, &c.—She prefented all thefe rarities to *Gebirus*, which he willingly receieved, and afterwards enquired what anfwer fhe brought to his fuit.—" Great King," faid " fhe, " My miftrefs is fenfible of your va- " lour and merit, and is far from refufing " fo advantageous an offer; but fhe muft " wait for a proper time, before fhe can re- " ward your love according to your de- " ferts.—The nobility are jealous of a fo- " reign prince; and fhe muft manage with " them fo as to bring them to agree, and to " receive you as their fovereign lord; in the " mean time you muft fhew readinefs to obey " all her commands;—to refide where fhe " fhall appoint, and to do what fhe fhall re- " quire, and fhe will take care to provide for " you and your fervants." He returned for
answer

anſwer.—" If ſhe will receive me for her huſ-
" band, I am ready to obey her commands
" in all things; and if the nobility refuſe to
" accept me for a King, let her call upon me,
" and I will compel them to her will:—and
" tell her for a marriage gift, I will bring
" her whatever ſhe pleaſes to aſk of me."—
" My Queen," replied this cunning ambaſ-
ſadreſs, " needs not any thing of yours,
" ſeeing, that all the riches on both ſides, will
" henceforward be in common between you:
" but while ſhe is employed in promoting
" your intereſt and happineſs, ſhe deſires that
" inſtead of a marriage preſent, you will
" cauſe a city to be built on that ſide next the
" great ſea, that it may be an honorable mark
" of your affection to her even to the end of
" the world.—And that it may be a diſco-
" very of your great power, and ſtrength, ſhe
" would have you employ in this work, thoſe
" great ſtones and pillars, which ſhe is in-
" formed you brought to dam up the chan-
" nel of the *Nile*;—by this you will give
" proof of your good intentions towards

　　　　　　　" the

" the inhabitants of *Ægpt*, and you will gain
" their love and duty towards you.—
" Moreover when this work is finished, she
" will over-rule all other difficulties, and
" make you her husband before all the
" world."

The King was exceeding glad at this pro-
posal, and granted her request.—And so it
was agreed between them that he should enter *Ægypt* on the west side, and that he should
found a city there; which was in the same
place where *Alexandria* now standeth. So
he encamped his army on the sea-side, and
Charoba sent provisions for him and his
people.

Now there were the ruins of a city in
that place, which city was founded by *Sedad*
the son of *Gad*, who was a great King, and
purposed to bring thither whatever was rare
and precious in all parts of the world. But
the destroyer of castles prevented him, even
Death, which none can escape or avoid.—
There were many remains of this ancient city,
and *Gebirus* caused to be brought thither, all
the

the stones and the pillars he had brought into
Ægypt.   And he assembled the engineers and
the artists from all those parts, and they made
a model for the new city; and *Charoba* sent
him a thousand workmen.   Now the nurse
who was *Charoba*'s confident, by her orders
consulted the magicians; and they by their
arts, employed certain demons of the sea, to
obstruct the buildings; so that *Gebirus* spent
a long time in building, and yet the city advanced very little: for whenever the buildings were nearly finished; while the workmen took their rest by night, the demons of
the sea came and pulled down the buildings,
and destroyed them; at which *Gebirus* was
greatly troubled and afflicted, until he understood the reason, by means of a strange
adventure that befel him.

Charoba had sent a thousand goats and
sheep, which were milked every day for the
King's kitchen.   They were kept by a young
shepherd to whom *Gebirus* gave the charge
of them,—he had other shepherds under him,

and

and they led their flocks out to graze every day by the sea-side.

Now the chief shepherd was a beautiful person, and of a goodly stature and aspect. One day when he had committed his flocks to the other shepherds, and wandered far away from them; he saw a fair young lady rising out of the sea, who walked towards him and saluted him graciously.—He returned her salutation and she began to converse with him.—"Young man,"—said she, "will you wrestle with me "for a wager that I shall lay against you?"— " What will you lay, fair lady," said the shepherd, " and what can I stake against you?"— " If you give me a fall," said the lady, " I " will be yours and at your disposal;—and if " I give you a fall, you shall give me a " a beast, out of your flock."—I am con- " tent,"—said the shepherd,—so he went to- towards her, and she met him, and wrestled with him, and presently gave him a fall. She then took a beast out of the flock, and car- ried it away with her into the sea.

She

She came every evening afterwards, and did the same, until the shepherd was desperately in love with her:—so the flock was diminished, and the shepherd was pining away with love and grief.

One day King *Gebirus*, passing by the shepherd, found him sitting very pensive by his flocks: so he came near and spoke to him.—" What misfortune hath befallen thee shep-" herd?—why art thou so altered and deject" ed?—thy flock also diminishes, and give" less milk every day?"—Upon this the shepherd took courage, and told the King all that had befallen him with the lady of the sea.—Which when *Gebirus* heard he was astonished, and in doubt whether to believe him.—" At what time," said he, " does this lady" visit thee?"—"Every evening," reply'd the shepherd, " when the sun is just ready to" set."—"Take off thy upper garment," said the King, " and thy bonnet also,—give" them to me, and retire thyself a little way" out of sight."—And the shepherd did so. So the

the King put on the shepherd's upper garment,
and his bonnet, and sat down in his place.

At the accustomed time, the young lady
came out of the sea, and saluted the King,
who returned her salutation.—" Wilt thou
" wreſtle any more with me upon the ſame
" terms?" ſaid ſhe.—" Yes with all my
" heart," ſaid the King. So he came towards
her, and gave her a fall preſently, and cruſh'd
her very much.—She cried out to him to ſpare
her, ſaying, " you are not my ordinary
" match."—" No," ſaid the King, " I am
" his maſter."—" Then," ſaid ſhe, " put me
" into his hands, ſince I am taken; for he
" has treated me courteouſly, and I have tor-
" mented his heart with love and grief:—
" mean time he hath captivated me, as I
" have him, and I will at laſt reward his
" love.—If thou wilt reſign me to my ſhep-
" herd, I will in requital, teach thee how to
" compleat thy buildings, and the city which
" thou haſt begun." He then promiſed to
give her to the ſhepherd, upon condition,
that ſhe would tell him from whence came
the

misfortunes that happened to his buildings, and the means whereby he might finish them. —" Know then Oh King!" said she, " that " this land of *Ægypt*, is full of magicians " and enchanters; and that the sea is full " of demons and spirits, which assist them to " carry on their affairs,—to build, and to de- " stroy. These are they who pull down thy " buildings, and obstruct thy city."—" And " what must I do to prevent them?"—said the King.

So she taught him to make certain statues of copper, and stone, and earth, and wood, and set them along by the sea-side, and she taught him to set spells upon them; so that when the demons of the sea came up to destroy the buildings, they saw the statues and returned back into the sea.

So she went and abode with the shepherd every day, but every night she returned in to the sea.

From this time, the buildings of *Gebirus* advanced, and he compleated many structures

as

as he had defired Then *Gebirus* had another conference with the lady of the fea, and he fpoke thus to her.

" Behold I have expended all the money
" that I brought hither, and the city is not
" yet finifhed, and I have no more money.
" Canft not thou difcover to me any hidden
" treafures in this land, whereby I may finifh
" my city, and not leave off my work to my
" difgrace and forrow."—The lady replied—
" There is much treafure in this ruined city
" and I will inftruct thee how to find it.—
" On the north fide of your buildings there is
" a round place,—on the outfide are feven
" pillars, with a brazen ftatue on the top of
" each of them.—Thou fhalt facrifice a fat bull
" to every one of thofe ftatues, and caufe the
" pillar under it to be rubb'd with the blood
" of the bull; then perfume it with the hair
" of his tail, and fhavings of his horns and
" hoofs. Then thou fhalt fay unto it,—
" Behold the offering I make to thee,—let
" me have that which is under thee, and
" about thee."—Having faid and done thus
" to every one of them meafure from every
                                    " pillar,

" pillar, on that side the face of the statue
" is turned towards, fifty cubits.—Then let
" thy people dig there.—You shall do all this
" when the moon is at the full.—After you
" have digged thirty cubits, you will find a
" great door; cause it to rubb'd with the
" gall of the bulls, and then take it away.—
" You shall then descend into a cave, fifty
" cubits in length. In it you will find a
" storehouse made fast with a lock, and the
" Key will be under the threshold of the door;
" take it and rub the door with the remain-
" der of the bulls galls, and perfume it with
" shavings of the horns and hoofs, and the
" hair of the tails, and then the door
" shall open.—You shall then wait a while,
" till the winds that are enclosed within
" get vent; and when they are calmed, you
" may enter. At the entrance, you will meet
" with a statue of brass, having about its
" neck, a plate of the same metal; on which
" is written a catalogue of all the treasures in
" these storehouses, of which you may take
" what you please. You shall make no stay
                                    " before

" before a dead perſon, whom you ſhall ſee
" there, laid upon a bed with regal orna-
" ments. Let not what is about him, of
" jewels and precious things, excite your en-
" vy or covetouſneſs; but, having taken
" away what is ſufficient for your occaſions,
" depart immediately; making faſt the doors,
" and covering the place with earth as you
" found it.—Know alſo that there are ſtore-
" houſes under every pillar and its ſtatue; for
" they are the tombs of ſeven Kings, who
" are buried there with all their treaſures.'

Gebirus was extremely ſatisfied with this
ccount which the nymph gave him; he
hanked her much, and went immediately,
and did all things that ſhe had ordered; and
he found immenſe wealth and treaſures, and
many rare and admirable things.—By theſe
means he completed the buildings of his
city.

When *Charoba* heard that the city was al-
moſt finiſhed, ſhe was afflicted, and fell into
great perturbation of mind; for ſhe meant
only to weary out the King, and to reduce
him to an impoſſibility.

After

After the city was finished, *Gebirus* sent some of his chief men, with the tidings to *Charoba*; and invited her to come and see it.—She was almost overwhelmed with grief and apprehension, that she should now be compelled to marry :—but her nurse comforted her with these words.—" Do not yet " despair, my royal mistress!—give not your- " self further trouble concerning this auda- " cious man.—Leave him to me, and I will ' shortly put it out of his power to give you " any further concern, or to do you mischief."

She returned with the messengers to *Gebirus*, and carried with her fine tapestry of great value, as a present from her mistress. —" Let this be put over the seat on which " the King sitteth," said she, " then let him " divide his people into three parties, and " send them forward to meet the Queen, who " will give them such treatment as they de- " serve. When the first party shall be about " a third part of the way, you shall send " away the second; and when the second " are got to their station, you shall send away

" the third:—thus they shall be dispersed
" about the country for the Queen's safety,
" and she shall have no cause to fear the de-
" signs of her enemies,—she will be attend-
" ed by the King's servants only, and when
" they return she will come with them."

So *Gebirus* sent away his servants, according to her instructions, and she continued
sending him rich presents every day, till such
time as she knew that the first party were arrived at their station.

Then by her orders there were tables set
before them covered with refreshments of all
kinds; but they were all poisoned meats.—
And while they sat down to eat; the Queen's
men and maid-servants stood all around them,
with umbrellas and fans to keep them cool;—
also their liquors were cooled.   So while they
sat at the tables they all died from the first to
the last.—Then the Queen's servants went
forwards to meet the second party, which they
treated in the same manner.—Then they removed to the third party, and served them as
they had done the others.—So the Queen's

servants

servants went forward; and a part of the Queen's army followed them, and they buried all the dead bodies.

Then the Queen, sent a message to the King, that she had left his army in and about her own city of *Masar*, and that she was coming to meet him speedily.—So she set forward with many attendants, and her nurse met her, and accompanied her to the city of the King.

When she drew near the palace, the King rose up, and went forward to meet her. Then the nurse threw over his shoulders a regal garment, which was poisoned, and which she had prepared for that purpose; afterwards she blew a fume into his face, which almost deprived him of his senses;—then she sprinkled him with a water that loosened all his joints, and deprived him of his strength; so that he fell down in a swoon at the feet of *Charoba*.—The attendants raised him up and seated him in a chair of state, and the nurse said unto him—" Is the King " well to night?"—He replied,—" A mischief on your coming hither!—may you be

I 2 " treated

" treated by others as you have treated me?—
" this only grieves me, that a man of ſtrength
" and valour ſhould be overcome by the ſub-
" tilty of a woman."—Is there any thing
" you would aſk of me before you taſte of
" death?" ſaid the Queen—" I would only
" intreat," ſaid he, " that the words I ſhall
" utter, may be engraven on one of the pil-
" lars of this palace which I have builded.

Then ſaid *Charoba*, " I give thee my pro-
" miſe that it ſhall be done; and I alſo will
" cauſe to be engraven on another pillar—
" This is the fate of ſuch men as would com-
" pel Queens to marry them, and kingdoms
" to receive them for their Kings."—Tell us
now thy laſt words.

Then the King ſaid—" I *Gebirus*, the *Me-*
" *taphequian*, the ſon of *Gevirus*, that have
" cauſed marbles to be poliſhed,—both the
" red and the green ſtone to be wrought curi-
" ouſly; who was poſſeſſed of gold, and jew-
" els, and various treaſures; who have raiſed
" ed armies; built cities; erected palaces;—
" who have cut my way through mountains;
                              " have

" have stopped rivers; and done many great
" and wonderful actions;—with all this my
" power, and my strength, and my valour,
" and my riches: I have been circumvented
" by the wiles of a woman; weak, impotent,
" and deceitful; who hath deprived me of
" my strength and understanding; and fi-
" nally hath taken away my life:—Where-
" fore, whoever is desirous to be great and
" to prosper; (though there is no certainty
" of long success in this world,)—yet, let
" him put no trust in a woman; but let
" him, at all times, beware of the craft and
" subtilty of a woman."

After saying these words, he fainted away,
and they supposed him dead; but after some
time he revived again.—*Charoba* comforted
him, and renewed her promise to him.—Being at the point of death, he said,—" Oh
" *Charoba!*—triumph not in my death!—for
" there shall come upon thee a day like unto
" this, and the time is not very far distant.—
" Then shalt thou reflect on the vicissitudes
" of fortune, and the certainty of death."—

Soon

Soon after this he expired.—*Charoba* ordered his body to be honorably interred in the city which he had builded.—Afterwards, she built an high tower in the same city; and caused to be engraven upon it her own name, and that of *Gebirus*: and an history of all that she had done unto him, and also those his last words.—So her fame went forth, and came to the ears of many Kings, and they feared and respected her. And she received many offers of friendship and alliance; but *Charoba* remained a virgin to the end of her life.

Now it happened about three years after the death of *Gebirus*, that *Charoba* having embarked on board a small vessel, in which she was wont to take her pleasure upon the *Nile* by moon-light; went on shore with some of her attendants.

As they were returning to the ship, with great mirth and jollity, it so happened that the Queen trod upon a serpent; which turned again, and stung her in the heel; the pain whereof, took away her sight.—Her women
comforted

comforted her,—saying, it would be nothing.
—" You are deceived," said she.—" The
" day is come with which *Gebirus* threatened
" me :—a day which all the great ones of the
" earth must meet and submit to.—Carry me
" home immediately, that I may die there."

The day following *Charoba* died ;—having
first appointed *Dalica*, her kinswoman to suc-
ceed her.—She was the daughter of that kins-
man, whom *Charoba* preserved from the cruelty of her father *Totis*.

So died *Charoba*, Queen of *Ægypt*; but
her name died not with her, for it remaineth,
and is honoured unto this day.

Queen *Dalica*, was endowed with beauty
and wisdom.—She followed the example of
her predecessor, and governed her kingdom
with great prudence.—She did many great
works in *Ægypt*,—and caused many castles
to be erected on the frontiers of the kingdom, to repel her enemies on whatever
side they should be attacked. She caused
the body of *Charoba*, to be embalmed with
camphire and spices ; and it was carried into
the

the city of *Gebirus*: for *Charoba* had caused
her tomb to be prepared there in her life-
time, and embellished it with regal ornaments, and appointed priests to attend on it.

Queen *Dalica* solemnized the funeral of
Charoba with great magnificence. She made
her subjects rich and happy by her wise government; and, after reigning seventy years
in *Ægypt*, died also a virgin, and was suc-
ceeded by her sister's son, *Ablinos*, whose posterity wore the crown of *Ægypt* for many gene-
rations.

F I N I S.

[*Entered at Stationers Hall.*]